THE TEFLON KID

From Wayward Youth To Eminent PhD Toxicologist

HOW THE HELL DID IT HAPPEN?

Francis X. Kamienski, PhD

BOOKSIDE Press

BOOKSIDE Press

BookSide Press
877-741-8091
www.booksidepress.com
orders@booksidepress.com

CONTENTS

Introduction   1
Love Life   3
Grandparents   3
Parents   5
Demographics   6
Ethnic Diversity   6
Early And Post-Depression Times   8
Victory Gardens   9
Early Life   10
Nicknames   10
Sophie's Boy   11
Adult Supervision   12
Outdoor Activities   13
The American Dream   14
Raiding Gardens   15
Pepsee (Pepsi)   16
Grade School   17
School Grades   19
Public School Defection   21
Altar Boy   22
Altar Boy & Weddings   25
Priest/Nun Vocations   26
Movie Theaters   27
Jobs Summary   27
    8-12 Years Old   28
    12-15 Years Old   30
    15-18 Years Old   33
Hopping Trains/Pumpkin Harvest Time   38
Floating The River   39
Sweet Tooth   40
Free Fireworks   41

Free Winter Tires   43
Free Gasoline   44
Shop Lifting   45
Winter Sledding   47
Teen Age Drinking   48
Drag Race Drinking   50
Keg Parties   51
Weekend Drinking   53
Automobile History   54
1934 Plymouth   54
1948 Ford   56
1953 Chevrolet   56
1949 Chevrolet   58
1953 Chevrolet   58
1970 Ford Station Wagon   59
Jamestown, New York   60
A Prom Night To Forget   62
Jail Times   64
    Oil City   64
    Titusville   65
    Franklin   66
Forest Ranger   67
Utah State 1958-1962   69
    Housing   69
    Freshman Year   71
    Sophomore Year   72
    Junior/Senior Years   72
College Jobs   73
Fish & Wild Life Check Station   73
Frat House Meals   74
Fighting Forest Fires   74

Bee Hive Transfers   76
Animal Husbandry Aide   76
Sorority House Hashing   76
USDA Animals Affecting Man And Animals   77
Serendipity   78
Student Loans   79
College Student Drinking   80
    Utah State   80
    Oregon State University   81
Drug Dealing   82
UC Berkeley Graduate School   83
Tom Robinson – Remember Him?   84
Dr. Casida – A Mentor   84
Harvard School Of Public Health   85
Professional Experience   86
Trophy Business   87
University Of California Medical School   89
Meeting U.S. Presidents   90
Ronald Reagan   90
George H. Walker Bush, The Elder   91
Polish Cooking - After Thoughts   92
Regressing And Reminiscing   93
Reflections   95

THE
TEFLON KID

From Wayward Teen To How
The Hell Did I Succeed

INTRODUCTION

You might ask - why am I writing this book. Well, many people have written bio books about themselves so why can't I. For instance, look at James Patterson's newest book – a bio about himself. Probably another best seller. While this book will not be a best seller why would I think that writing about my adventures (or misadventures) would interest anyone in my trials and tribulations? Primarily, because I believe my life is not considered mainstream. People that didn't grow up like I did in the 40's and 50's, who grew up without a father, who didn't face the challenges of my generation and environment, will realize after reading my book, that they may have missed out on many exciting and unusual experiences in their youth.

The situations I encountered - and endured – are probably atypical of youths growing up in my times or compared to the youth of today who are mesmerized with electronic gadgets, Snapchat, Tik-Tok, video games, etc. and other distractions.

I further believe my life story is unique because of my background, upbringing, and twists and turns that befuddled me from my early youth growing up without a father and raised in a Polish ghetto in a small western Pennsylvania town of Oil City.

As you read on, you will discover actions in my preteens, teens and even events in my college days might have had dire consequences had I been caught. Remember John Gotti, the mafia boss who was titled the Teflon Don. He managed for years to avoid prosecution for murder, extortion, tax evasion, etc.; However, the law eventually caught up with him. Hence the title of The Teflon Kid. It reminds me how lucky I was for not getting caught for many of my escapades.

I have hidden these stories from my wife Patty of 55 years. When I begin to mention some exploits, she didn't wish to hear about them. So, I have no one to tell them to – except for now – you. Probably a good thing. I would be ashamed to have her know the intimate details of some of my less than proud experiences. Had she known about my past she may have questioned my ideals and never married me.

Initially, I wished to shield my stories from my sons and family – and some friends. They have a respected image of me and I wished to keep it as such. I didn't want them to get an inkling that it might be I who is the person writing this book. However, on second thought I said hell – I am what I am, and I did what I did so why hide it. This writing should fill them in.

Please note the chronology of this book periodically skips from one age, subject or time period to another. I found that grouping my activities by periods or subjects gives the reader a better depiction of my experiences.

As you read through the book, please understand that: (1) I had little or no supervision during my growing up years (2) I'm an energetic type "A" personality and (3) I never had a goal in life and meandered from one experience to another.

The narratives expounded in this book are true based on my recollections/experiences. Some names have been changed to protect the innocent from shame (and myself from the not so innocent) as they might want retribution or payback for name dropping! Because of this, I wish to remain anonymous. Hell, if I didn't change names, I'd have to enroll in the Witness Protection Program.

LOVE LIFE

James Patterson's latest book goes into details of his first kiss, etc. To tell you the truth, I don't remember my first kiss or my second kiss. I intentionally spare the reader of details and do not mention or delve into any aspect of my romantic experiences. Some were boring some not. Either way they are not included. Although there were episodes that had many wild twists – all ending in being married to my wonderful and loving wife Patty for 45 years.

GRANDPARENTS

I mention my grandparents, especially my grandmother, because she was very influential in my upbringing. She impacted on me the benefits of hard work and persistence for survival in the real world. I discuss my interactions with her later on.

My grandparents came separately to America on boats from Poland as young teens. My grandmother came from Eastern Poland near the German border. I learned of her origin later in her life as she lay bedridden only because I had a German class in college and her mention of Germany that crept into our conversation. I have no idea of my grandfather's origin mainly because we had little interaction and he passed early in my life.

My grandparents met in Fredonia, New York, got married and ended up in Oil City. Other than them having relatives in Buffalo, upstate New York and Detroit, I know nothing about their experiences in coming to America and their early hardships. In retrospect, I wish

I could have asked them – and likewise my mom - more about their adventures and experiences not only here but also in Europe.

Neither grandparent spoke a word of English when they arrived in America – and spoke none until the day they died. Neither grandparent could even read Polish. I was constantly asked to read letters from relatives in Poland and the Polish newspapers grandma routinely received from the old country. Needless to say, my grasp of the Polish language was very good. So good that on occasions I was asked to compose letters to her relatives that she dictated to me.

Even though the Polish neighborhood elders spoke no English there was no need for them to do so. There were five Polish run grocery stores, two Polish Clubs (drinking bastions) and four neighborhood taverns or "beer gardens". We even had a Catholic Church where sermons were primarily delivered in Polish. In addition, my mom and her generation spoke both Polish and English. They were intermediates in the network of communications between all age groups in the neighborhood.

Speaking of church, our local Polish church had three morning Masses. The majority of elder people attended the two earlier Masses because sermons were in Polish. The sermon in the later Mass was usually delivered in English. As time went on and the elderly parishioner population dwindled, all the sermons were delivered in English. Not sure this was a blessing as sermons were quite boring and uninspiring even in English.

While grandma spoke no English, she was a fabulous cook. She prepared Polish food to die for. She loved to cook for her grandson Naniu (me). She was a much better cook than my mother or her two sisters.

PARENTS

I was raised without a father. My parents were divorced when I was three. I never saw my dad and have no recollection of him even though he lived nearby. Truth is I never had a desire to meet him after what my mom told me about him. She rarely mentioned him only saying he was a "womanizer". Guess that pretty much explains who he was and why my parents got divorced.

On one occasion, my mom said my father was coming to visit and wanted to see me. For whatever reason I dodged the opportunity. Probably because I was upset of the fact that he abandoned me and I didn't wish to forgive him. I'm sure life for me would have been very different with a dad.

After the divorce, my mom faced hardships and struggled to raise me. Early on she went to beauty school and did hair but work was sporadic. Eventually she found full time employment in a glass factory. Their biggest productions were milk bottles since at that time all milk was sold in glass bottles. They also manufactured baby and perfume bottles etched with distributor logos. The plant environment was pretty hot from the molten glass poured into molds. She worked there for minimum wage for about 30 years.

Even though I disliked my father, hats off to him for he religiously sent her a monthly child support check of $30 (I know this because I serendipitously opened a letter from him to my mom and saw the check). But let me tell you even with these monthly checks raising a kid on minimum wage was tuff!

Enough about no father.

DEMOGRAPHICS

Oil City, a rural town in Western Pennsylvania, was and still is a working-class blue color town. Oil was a big industry in early Western Pennsylvania. Initially the source of oil used in the early days came from surface pools. Oil and oil products at that time were mainly used for lighting and heating purposes. It wasn't until 1850 when Colonel Francis Drake drilled the first oil well in Titusville, eight miles from town that production greatly increased. The coincidental development of the auto industry sparked an oil boom which greatly benefited our area.

Pennsylvania crude oil was in great demand for use in auto engines because of the high boiling point. It was preferred over Oklahoma or Texas crude since it withstood high engine temperatures and did not readily break down.

Not surprising many people were employed by Quaker State, Pennzoil and Wolf's Head Oil Refineries built in or near our town. There were other industries in our area that also employed many people; i.e., two steel factories, two glass plants and three chemical plants but oil was king.

ETHNIC DIVERSITY

Growing up, Oil City we had a population of about 15,000 somewhat divided into a mix of nationalities. The majority ethnic group were the "English" as my mom and others called them. Our Polish neighborhood was the major minority. It was actually a closed knit ghetto of "Pollacks" where everyone knew everybody. There were fewer number of minorities in the city such as the Irish, Italians, Jewish - and three black families - but we predominated. I lived in "Pollack Hill" as my neighborhood was called.

This was the time in the 30's and early 40's where ethnic groups kept to themselves, minded their own business and did not trust or respect each other. They seldom strayed from their neighborhoods. Talk about ethnic bias. As an example, my grandmother told me if I ever married an Italian woman, she would disown me. Personally, I never had anything against Italians – nor did I marry one. In fact, one of my best friends was a Paisano named Guy subsequently mentioned several times later on. I'm sure you get the flavor of these ethnic relationships back in those days.

Ethnic boundaries were quite distinct and initially, outsiders were not tolerated. My high school history teacher said he sold insurance before becoming a teacher. He said you didn't dare wander into a Polish neighborhood and said I quote "if you didn't want the shit beat out of you". Of course, we were not threatened if we wandered in other English neighborhoods since they had no idea of our Polish ethnicity.

As time went on ethnicity issues abated. There were still some ethnicity concerns when I began high school, but they quickly diminished as time went on. In fact, my best high school friends included Irish, Italian and Jewish kids - and surprising few Pollacks.

In fact, the largest and best attended event in the tri-city area was the annual "Polish Picnic" Outsiders scarfed up the kapusta (sauerkraut), kielbasa, pierogi (Polish pot stickers), golabki (pigs in the blanket) and other Polish delights that were served as evidenced by their large attendance. A band provided dancing music – of course, mostly Polish. Card and dice games were played by elder men. Without saying, the booze flowed and there were always skirmishes especially at the poker table.

EARLY AND POST-DEPRESSION TIMES

Even without a grasp of the English language, my grandparents successfully raised eight kids – five boys and three girls. During the war, my grandfather worked in a steel factory that produced shell casings for the war effort. I was told that even with his English language barrier he worked for 6 years in the factory. Apparently, there was a Polish-English bilingual manager who was liaison between my grandfather and other nonspeaking Polish-speaking workers.

In the early forties, manufacturing of war-related materials was in full swing—an all-out effort for Americans to support the war. My mom even worked two years in a plant making shell casings.

To provide food for the family during the Depression, my grandparents were quite industrious. My grandmother had a chicken coop which provided eggs and chicken products. They had three milk cows. My oldest uncle Mike was a "cow puncher". Each day he would take the cows into the hills and let them graze for a few hours. Don't know what my other uncles did during these times but all three girls (my mom and two aunts) either did hair or worked as house maids.

Bottom line: my grandparents did a great job raising the family through the Depression era.

As an aside all five uncles served in the armed forces during the war. In fact, my uncle Mickey was in the Navy shooting pool in Honolulu when the Japanese attacked Pearl Harbor. He sustained a shoulder injury from a bullet but survived. Uncle Walter was in the merchant marines and survived a U-boat attack on one of his ships. The other boys were in the army.

VICTORY GARDENS

During the war many when food items were scarce, Polish folks in the neighborhood had "Victory Gardens" where they grew all kinds of vegetables. The most popular vegetable was cabbage which ended up as sauerkraut after fermenting in vinegar over the winter in wooden keg barrels. While my grandmother had no Victory Garden in her back yard, there were apple, cherry and peach trees along with grapes on the property from which she made jellies and wines. Occasionally I sneaked tastes of the wines—they were smooth and high in alcohol content. Glad I kept my pilfering to a few sips.

In addition to the back yard fruit sources, my grandparents owned small plot of land about 1/16 of an acre. Here the family grew beans, beets, cabbage (what else), broccoli, brussels sprouts, cauliflower, carrots, horseradish, lettuce, peas, potatoes, pumpkins, radishes and watermelons. Many of these items were canned or processed for later consumption. Nothing went to waste.

You might say I too was a farmer. I was very familiar with the hard work involved in planting and gardening. Each spring my Uncle Mike and I would prepare the ground for planting – not with a rototiller but with pitchforks. I started working this plot at twelve years of age. It was an annual chore. It took Uncle Mike and I about two full days to prepare the ground for plantings. Another couple days were needed for planting. Talk about hard work!

However, the plus side was that times were booming during and after WW II. Post war times were especially good! Seems like everyone was working and had money to spend. Over time demand of products from the backbone war industries waned. Eventually these industries closed up shop and moved down South and other places for cheaper labor.

EARLY LIFE

My recollection of family life probably started at about three years old. Initially my mom and I lived in a small one room apartment for two years. This was followed by living with my uncle's family (three girls, two boys and three adults) in a small three bed room house. This lasted less than a year as the overcrowded situation was not conducive to any degree of privacy or from an unpredictable head of their household – my dear old Uncle Nick who occasionally drank more than his share. Subsequently my mom rented a small apartment for the two of us. Three years later my grandfather passed and we moved in with my grandmother at age six.

I was basically raised by my grandmother - as well as by my aunts, uncles, mom's friends and others in the neighborhood, i.e., in essence raised by the "village".

NICKNAMES

Growing up in our Polish neighborhood, nicknames were commonplace. How or when most originated are not known but many folks had them. There were, however, one appropriately nicknamed individual, i.e., Stinky, who was known to regularly flatulate in class and then point a finger at innocent students. His nickname should have been Sneaky.

My nickname was Mince for short or Mince Meat. To this day I'm still called Mince or Mincer by many of my friends when they greet me even though I haven't seen some of them in over 60 years.

Other neighborhood nicknames included Barney, Bashu, Bogie, Bosco, Butzek, Chops, Cooper, Cuddy, Frenchie, Footsie, Gussie, Guy, Hatchett Nose (man what a Schnoze), Hugo, Izzy, Jazz, Jimma, Juggar, Leaping Leo, Marty, Maumau (a mute), Mayor Mike, Muzzy, Naniu (my Polish nickname), Peeker, Pokey, Pootang, Reba, Rudy, Schooner, Sobo, Spooks, Stasiu, Peaches, Smaltz, Tex, Zach, Ziggy and of course my best friend Pepsee (Pepsi). These nicknames sort of reminds one of "Our Gang" characters – aka Alfalfa, Buckwheat, Spanky, etc., Coincidentally, we had a guy nick named Buckwheat in our neighborhood.

Rarely did girls or women in our community have nicknames. Might this be classified as gender discrimination?

SOPHIE'S BOY

I was also known in the neighborhood as "Sophies" boy. Folks knew I had no dad and were very nice to me probably because of my family situation but more so because my mom was well known, liked, and respected in our community. Folks occasionally invited me to their homes for Polish meals and other treats. They also reprimanded me when required. Somewhat akin to being raised by the "village".

While not growing up in true ghetto like Dr. Ben Carson, who grew up in the poorest area of Detroit to become a famous neurosurgeon, I likewise had to navigate through obstacles in my Polish environment, overcome experiences and situations to achieve what I accomplished later in life. I relate in detail how I evaded blame for many troublesome episodes I was involved in growing up and how I eventually salvaged my life to graduate from four universities - Utah State (Bachelor of Arts), Oregon State (Master of Arts), U.C Berkeley (PhD in Toxicology) and the Harvard School of Public Health (Post Doctorate Drug Research).

I never planned on being a perpetual student but I attended college for twelve consecutive years. The student tenure wasn't because of evading the draft in the 60's or running from anything – it was because of a burning hunger to learn more!

ADULT SUPERVISION

You could say that I had supervision (from grandma and the nuns) but you could also say I didn't have a lot.

While growing up my mom worked in a glass factory. She worked rotating shifts - day, night and swing shifts. I was instructed to be home by 10:00 when my mom worked the night shift. She left home a little later to go to work. As soon as she left, I hit the streets and played with the older boys in the neighborhood and came home when the group disbanded usually close to midnight. Grandmother never said much about my sneaking out since she went to bed early.

Once I hit high school age, I was pretty much free to roam as I pleased with no curfew or other restrictions except to stay out of trouble. I tried to do that but failed miserably!

One might surmise from reading my early adventures that I was on a path of juvenile delinquency or self-destruction. Over time, I somehow avoided consequences of my actions. I was involved in many unusual things - some which might have normally led to punitive measures for my behavior if caught. How I escaped accountability and punishments for most of my actions – just plain luck, I guess. A true Teflon Kid!

My upbringing by caring people like my Polish grandmother, relatives and our neighborhood friends guided me through my uncertain youthful days when I needed mentoring the most. From them, I was entombed with the rewards of hard work and persistence.

Had it not been for these folks, I might not be the person I now am or the success I achieved in my lifetime.

OUTDOOR ACTIVITIES

I developed an early interest in camping, fishing and hunting. I had no dad, or relatives interested in the outdoors. I had no one to mentor me in outdoors activities. I recall my first fishing experience quite vividly. When I was six, I pestered Uncle Mike – who was the furthest person from an outdoorsman - to take me fishing. I only caught a small trash fish "chub" that day but I was hooked on fishing. However, Uncle Mike never took me fishing again so I was on my own again.

The Alleghany River flowed through Oil City. Myself and several friends would routinely wade into the river and fish the riffles for chubs. We would normally catch over a hundred of the critters a day and throw them back. There were other fish to be caught – bass and walleyes which were great eating.

At that time, raw sewage was diverted directly into the lower portion of the river in our town. Fish caught above the effluent were okay to eat. I caught my largest fish - a 4-lb bass in the effluent – a real trophy - but unfortunately threw it back. Oh - once I slipped and fell into the sewage effluent; went home and discarded all my clothing.

As I grew older and before of age to drive, I pestered Joe Hajduk, an older neighbor to take me fishing. Many times, after Joe's work, I waited at his house hoping for an invite to go fishing. Fortunately, he was able to take me most of the time. How could he resist. I always awaited him with my fishing gear.

Joe eventually bought a farm. I also pestered him to take me hunting for small game on his farm after his work - which he did.

He also seeded my desire for deer hunting which I still do today. From Joe's mentoring, the outdoors were engrained in my DNA.

THE AMERICAN DREAM

Talk about the American Dream. Other than loving hunting and fishing I had none. I was a happy boy and only looked forward to the adventures the next day would present. Basically, I was like a lost deer in the head lights with no aim or goal in life. I had no idea what I wanted to be or do when I grew older. I never wanted to be a fireman, policeman, pilot or any other achiever. Many of my friends likewise had no ambitions or premonitions to become someone or accomplish something in life. In fact, very, very few of them went to college.

Having a goal in life reminds me of my brother-in-law Dr. Samuel Butler. He was a well-known cardiovascular surgeon at Loyola University in Chicago who said he wanted to be a doctor when he was four years old. In other words, he had a goal very early in life – something to shoot for. Perhaps his career vision was influenced by both his parents who were medical doctors.

Conversely, I had no dad or mentor to guide me in my early years. How I overcame my wandering life and other travesties and became an educational success as a PhD biochemist and toxicologist from two of the greatest universities in America is a story in itself!

Bottom line - if I could salvage my life and achieve this level of achievement, anyone could in our great country! As they say anything is possible to achieve and live the American Dream – if you work for it. I overcame many obstacles, worked hard for it and earned it!

More on this subject later.

I had many chores while living with my grandparents. I was assigned to collect eggs from the chicken coop, clean out chicken manure from the hen house, assist in the gruesome process of sacrificing and plucking chickens, mow lawns, paint and periodically whitewash of the concrete house foundation when these needs arose. The worse task occurred once a year in the fall when Uncle Mike and I would carry a ton - yes one ton - of dumped coal from the street up the 15 or so steps to the house in straw bushel baskets. This was a two-day back breaking affair. After I left for college, my younger cousins were recruited for this chore.

Did I mention I never received any compensation for the chores I performed around the house? These chores encroached on the time I could have done money-earning chores elsewhere. What a bummer. But as I relate later this didn't prevent me from making spending money.

RAIDING GARDENS

During the war many people in our neighborhood had "Victory Gardens". They evolved out of necessity as many foods were not available during the war. In the summers and fall, my friends and I would "raid" Victory Gardens at night and dine on the spoils, i.e., cabbage, cucumbers, beans and fruits – you name it - we stole it and ate it.

I quit raiding gardens after one episode. I once removed radishes from a neighbor's yard. They had a funny taste. Turns out the funny taste was chicken manure since it and cow manure were commonly used as fertilizers in neighborhood gardens. Apparently, the manure was absorbed through the roots by the radishes. As you might guess my raiding gardens were desisted from future excursions.

On one occasion I had serious stomach pains which they thought was appendicitis. I was scared to death of getting operated on and fought tooth and nail about going to the hospital. After several tests and examinations, they concluded I had gas in my bowel which was causing the intense pain. They further concluded the symptoms were probably due to eating green apples. What a relief.

PEPSEE (PEPSI)

Who the hell is Pepsee?

It would be derelict of me not to include mention of my best friend Pepsee. He was truly a boyhood mentor who had a profound influence on me growing up. He was a year older, lived in the neighborhood and attended the Assumption of the Blessed Virgin Mary parochial school – as I did. He had an uncanny ability to develop schemes to steer us into potential trouble.

Aside from the above, Pepsee was a great athlete in high school. He excelled in basketball and football. However, baseball was by far his greatest skill and liking. Unfortunately, there was no baseball program in our high school – only our summer Little League. His love of baseball was such that he spent countless hours fielding grounders and rebounding ground balls thrown against a wall. He was a determined soul.

Pepsee excelled in Little League baseball and was his team's star shortstop. In fact, his 12-year-old team played in the Little League World Series in Williamsport. I'm sure his talents helped his team get there. Unfortunately, his team did not advance to the championship game.

After high school, he had tryouts with several pro teams including the Pittsburgh Pirates, his favorite team. Scouts from the several teams were interested in him and wanted to see his skills. His baseball dream terminated when after several tryouts with different teams he was not offered a roster spot. Incidentally, he was offered a baseball scholarship from Northwestern. Unfortunately, low grades precluded his entrance to the university.

It was hard to believe he wasn't drafted. He definitely had the talent. I played against him in little league saw him play a lot in the older leagues. Hell, there wasn't much more to do than watch baseball games. Recently, I asked him if our high school had a baseball program and/or if he played college baseball might that have resulted in honing his skills and enhance his chance of making the pros. He said definitely, it probably would have.

Nonetheless, he was quite successful in life. Went to night school. Got a degree. President of his local Chamber of Commerce, Chairman of the March of Dimes and involved in many local activities. Since retired, he now spends time between homes in Erie, Pa and Florida. He moved to Florida not only for the mild winter weather but also to be near the Vero Beach spring training sites of several pro baseball teams. To this day he plays softball with the older fellas and says he's still a pretty good infielder.

As an aside, I promised not to delve into my love life but I lied. I neglected to mention that besides being a gifted athlete, Pepsee was also a good looking hunk. Why do I mention this? Well, on one occasion I was making points with a girl from Franklin – and was doin' pretty good until Pepsee moved in and pushed me out of the picture. He moved in on me again with another girl I was smitten with. I mean what the hell are friends for! Turns out both girls dumped us for other dudes. Justice served.

GRADE SCHOOL

As previously mentioned, I attended the Assumption BVM school (located two houses from ours) from grades 1 through 8. We were taught by nuns – strict and somewhat mean. Discipline was king.

Beatings for misconduct or not doing lessons was the rule of the day. Some of the beatings were not pleasant. Guess they weren't meant to be.

One particular form of punishment was hitting fingers with the metal edge of a ruler. Damn that was painful. Another favorite was to twist and pinch your cheek causing you to stand up. Or lastly, depending on your teacher, a good ear twist was forthcoming.

Worse part of the punishment was if you went home and complained to your parents that the nuns beat you then a second beating was bestowed on you from parents for misbehaving in school. Relating school discipline episodes to parents – uh-uh - mum was the word.

I remember two occasions when I knew the hurt was coming and advised to go to the principal's office. It was the custom if capital punishment was required. They would march us to the principal's office. If the principal visits were known ahead of time, I would wear thick corduroy pants to deflect the sting from the principal's stick – which on occasion we hid from her. Drove her up the wall! Once I put a towel in my corduroy britches and feigned pain and cried just to stop the beating. I'm telling you the principal was one mean servant of God who took great pleasure in beating students. On rare occasions even girls did not escape her wrath.

As you may have guessed one of the school subjects was Religion. In fact, it was the first subject. The second was Polish - which was abandoned when I was in the third grade. The Catholic church I attended (three houses from mine) had services in Latin and sermons in Polish. Nothing in English! Since raised by my Polish grandmother - who spoke no English and conversed with me exclusively in Polish - I was probably one of the few kids, who could understand the sermons – not that this was any great benefit to me. With mass in Latin and sermons in Polish how the hell was one to enjoy going to Mass. This drudgery lasted for 18 years until I left town for college.

SCHOOL GRADES

My elementary school grades were very excellent! I was usually ranked #1 in the class of 14 throughout my eight years. A copy of one of my grade school report cards are illustrated below (Figures 1 and 2).

ASSUMPTION BVM GRADE I

SUBJECTS	FIRST SEMESTER				SECOND SEMESTER			
	First Period	Second Period	Third Period	Sem.	Fourth Period	Fifth Period	Sixth Period	Sem.
RELIGION	S	S	S	98	S	S	S	100
READING	S	S	S	100	S	S	S	100
NUMBERS	S	S	S	94	S	S	S	100
LANGUAGE		S	S	100	S	S	S	95
SPELLING		S	S	100	S	S	S	100
WRITING	S	S	S	90	S	S	S	95
MUSIC	S	S	S	95	S	S	S	85
ART	S	S	S	90	S	S	S	95
HEALTH	S	S	S	90	S	S	S	85
Polish Reading	S	S	S	100	S	S	S	100

The check mark indicates the reading level at the time of the Report — Is reading at pre-primer level ✓
Is doing work preparatory to reading ✓ — Is reading at first reader level ✓
Is reading at the primer level ✓ — Is reading at second reader level ✓

ATTENDANCE RECORD

Days excused absence	1	2	0	0	0	8	1	9
Days unexcused absence	0	0	0	0	0	0	0	0
Days in attendance period	30	30	30	90	30	30	30	90
Times Tardy	0	0	0	0	0	1	0	0

Tardy bells ring at 8:50 a.m., and 1:00 p.m.
Morning session closes at 12:00 noon.
Afternoon session closes at 3:30 p.m.

Parents are urged to insist that their children observe the Rules of Safety on the way to and from school.

EXPLANATION OF SUBJECT MARKS
... has done excellent work in subject.
... has done satisfactory work.
... has not met minimum requirements of subject.

Figure 1

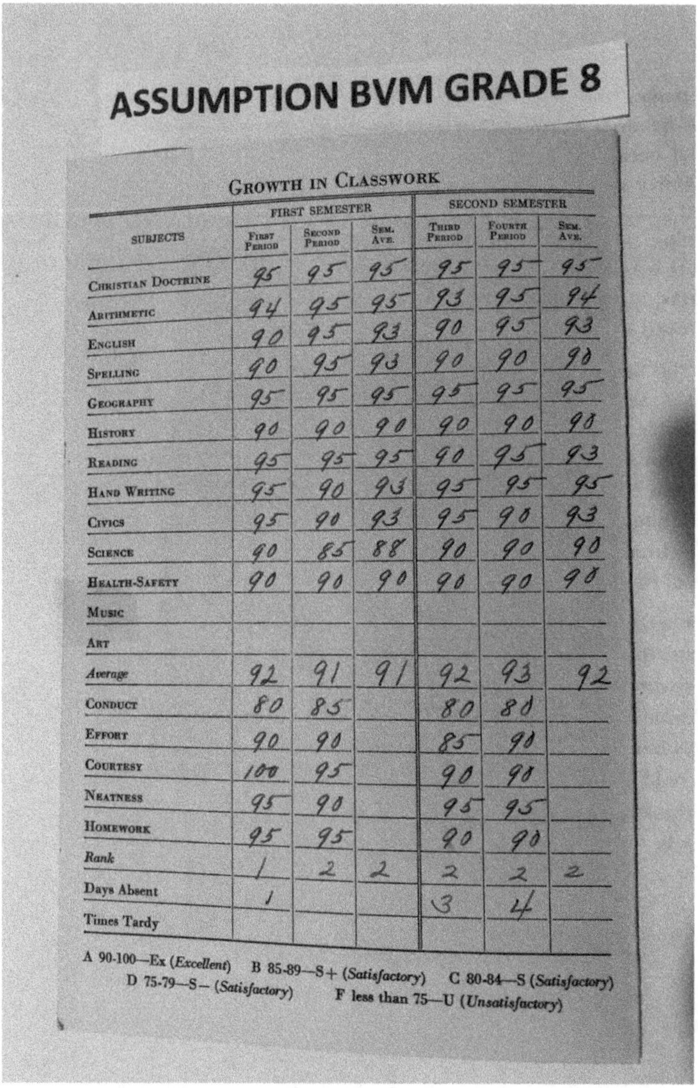

ASSUMPTION BVM GRADE 8

GROWTH IN CLASSWORK

SUBJECTS	FIRST SEMESTER			SECOND SEMESTER		
	First Period	Second Period	Sem. Ave.	Third Period	Fourth Period	Sem. Ave.
Christian Doctrine	95	95	95	95	95	95
Arithmetic	94	95	95	93	95	94
English	90	95	93	90	95	93
Spelling	90	95	93	90	90	90
Geography	95	95	95	95	95	95
History	90	90	90	90	90	90
Reading	95	95	95	90	95	93
Hand Writing	95	90	93	95	95	95
Civics	95	90	93	95	90	93
Science	90	85	88	90	90	90
Health-Safety	90	90	90	90	90	90
Music						
Art						
Average	92	91	91	92	93	92
Conduct	80	85		80	80	
Effort	90	90		85	90	
Courtesy	100	95		90	90	
Neatness	95	90		95	95	
Homework	95	95		90	90	
Rank	1	2	2	2	2	2
Days Absent	1			3	4	
Times Tardy						

A 90-100—Ex (*Excellent*)   B 85-89—S+ (*Satisfactory*)   C 80-84—S (*Satisfactory*)
D 75-79—S– (*Satisfactory*)   F less than 75—U (*Unsatisfactory*)

Figure 2

Because of my academic ratings, I escaped a lot of beatings. Classmates who weren't very smart and didn't know or do assignments went to the gallows. However, my constant need for attention resulted in dismal deportment grades – and subsequent whippings (refer to the report card).

The upside of my parochial school teachings was that in ninth grade in high school, I was essentially a grade level in learning above my classmates – as were my other classmates taught by nuns. Hell, we all made the honor roll in our freshman year. Because of our excellent parochial teachings, I rarely studied in high school and never learned to study.

In retrospect – the nuns were truly excellent teachers.

PUBLIC SCHOOL DEFECTION

In the early part of his seventh grade in Assumption, and having taken enough punishment from the nuns – which he probably deserved - Pepsee enrolled in the Lincoln Junior High School, a public institution. He told me how great it was at the new school. No nuns. Lax discipline. No homework. Fun. Why wouldn't he like it. Studying was not required since most of the nun teachings were above what was offered at Lincoln. He said why don't you enroll here. At least you would have a buddy in me.

He later told me his mom found about the transfer a month after enrolling. He said it was too late for her to do anything about it.

So, in the seventh grade with Pepsee's urging and without telling my mom, I enrolled in Lincoln Junior High. Pepsee was correct. Studies were easy and it was fun. Three days later, my mom found out about my defection. She read me the riot act and told to immediately go back to purgatory – which I did. Oh well, the experience was fun while it lasted. I thought if the public high school was like the taste of the Lincoln experience, I could look forward to enrolling there rather than at the Catholic High School after graduating from Assumption.

ALTAR BOY

Talk about religion. Mass was a daily ritual. However, during summer when school was over attending Mass for students was not required.

Altar boys were selected by the nuns usually in the third or fourth grade. Unlucky me. Either because I lived so close to the church or the nuns took a liking to me, I was anointed as an altar boy in the third grade.

I served altar boy duties for five years. At that time there was a pool of altar boys – no girls - who were rotated on weekly bases to serve Mass. Two boys served each Mass. Being an altar boy meant Mass attendance every day before school when your turn came about. What a drag. However, the upside was the prestige from serving.

Besides serving Mass during the school year, selected altar boys were also required to serve daily Mass every other week during the summer vacation. Another drag. The upside was that I had to rise early and had longer days to enjoy myself.

One would surmise that being an altar boy was an angelic blessing which resulted in halos around our heads from being so close to God. Well not so. There were capers – some not so religious.

During the Mass, the standard procedure was for altar boys to carry cruets of water and wine which on cue were poured into the chalice held by the priest. We knew where the wine was stored in the vestibule. Prior to Mass, the altar boys dressed in the basement and went upstairs to the vestibule to fill the cruets with wine and water before the priest showed up for the service. The wine was stored in an unlocked closet. Occasionally, after the ceremonies and after the priest left, we would help ourselves to a swig or two from the wine bottle(s).

Several priests were boozers. They sometimes had a drink of wine either before or after services – or sometime on both occasions.

They apparently had no idea that we slightly depleted their stocks. Great thing was we never got caught. I felt that even if we got caught some of the priests would not have said anything!

Prior to Mass the ritual was for altar boys to light candles with long sticks containing a lighted wick and a snuffer (Figure 3).

Figure 3

The Easter and Christmas ceremonies were very formal. There were six especially tall, ornately decorated candles on each side of the altar to light before the Mass. The lighting was to be a dignified synchronized process by each altar boy. This process usually took a few minutes and extreme care was required to light these tall candles.

After Mass the reverse ritual was to extinguish the candles with the snuffer again in a synchronized matter. However, sometimes the race was on – each altar boy trying to finish the extinguishing chore before the other. The nuns chastised us for rushing the extinguishing but nevertheless we continued the race - until once in my haste while extinguishing, I pulled down a lit candle and burned a hole on the altar linen. Needless to say, the nuns burned a hole in my behind.

After an unneeded beating by the nuns, I regressed to conducting extinguishing candles in a more dignified manner as required.

Passing the collection baskets occurred in the middle of the Mass. The money collections were originally assigned to altar boys. They presented baskets thru each row and collected the offerings. The baskets containing the money were then placed in the vestibule after the collection. The nuns came after each Mass to collect the offerings. One altar boy, name unmentioned, who I observed on several occasions, grabbed a handful of dollars from the collection baskets and stuffed them in his pocket. I didn't report him because of the emerta code – silence among bandidos. Also, I don't mention his name here as he still might come after me if I did. I'm proud to say I never stole any collection money. I also didn't know if other altar boys helped themselves to the collection money – I suspect some of them did.

However, the nuns were pretty sharp. They eventually caught on to the thievery. They subsequently assigned lay people to pass the baskets and keep the collections in a room in the back of the church. I trust none of them pilfered any monies.

Another prank during services was burning incense in a gold contraption i.e., Censer (Figure 4).

Figure 4

This gadget was to contain a single a red hot glowing special charcoal briquet prepared by altar boys during the Mass. The priest would then sprinkle incense with a small gold spoon onto the charcoal, swing the contraption while mumbling some prayers in Latin which no one understood. Smoke and a pleasant essence would emanate as the incense contacted the charcoal.

On several occasions, Pepsee and I used three briquets which when the incense contacted them resulted in an evolution of a great deal of smoke - damn near chocking the priest. After a couple episodes the nuns put a stop to these shenanigans enforcing the one briquet rule with a tongue lashing and of course a beating. Said if happened again we would not serve as altar boys. Even though I thought this was and idle threat this could have been my chance to retire from the ranks of altar boy duties. However, the prestige of being an altar boy and another perk (serving at weddings) overrode my desire to quit.

ALTAR BOY & WEDDINGS

During church wedding ceremonies, a single altar boy was assigned to assist the priest. The nuns rotated and assigned boys – unless the wedding party requested a specific altar boy. The nuns apparently favored me because I served at more weddings than others. And since I knew all people in the neighborhood – and they knew me, I had another advantage. I would approach either the bride or groom and ask them to request me as the altar boy. This presented an opportunity for me to serve at numerous weddings.

Not the end of the story. The custom for the wedding party was to provide envelopes (containing money) to both the priest conducting the ceremony and the altar boy after the service. The priest probably needed the money to buy booze. Most times the envelop for the altar boy contained one or two dollars – but occasionally a five-dollar bill appeared in the envelope. The nuns found out how the system worked and commandeered the altar boy's envelopes. The nuns then kept the paper money and gave 50 cents to the serving altar boy.

Knowing the nuns would help themselves to the money in the envelop, I would circumvent their greed by asking the wedding party to give me the envelop after the service outside of the church. This scenario worked for a while until the nuns realized that their revenue evaporated when I served. As you guessed, my serving time diminished and I was rarely selected to serve weddings unless the wedding party was a relation insisting on my service.

PRIEST/NUN VOCATIONS

Assumption being a parochial school, it was the intention of the nuns to brain wash us into serving the Lord. As eighth graders, toward the end of the year, our nun once asked the class with a show of hands who wanted to be either a priest or a nun. The nuns must have thought some of us had a calling. Nobody raised their hands. Guess all the constant punishments over eight years from the nuns thwarted our enthusiasm to serve the Lord. Our unanimous surprise rejections sent the nun on a tirade accompanied with extensive sermonizing which lasted about a week.

Besides rejecting priesthood or nun hood, not a single one of my classmates went to our Catholic High School; all opted to attend our public school. The nun freaked out! As it turns our only a few students from our school ever went to the Catholic High School. My older cousin went to the Catholic school but two of his three sisters did not. The brainwashing must have paid off as his third sister went into the convent after parochial school.

MOVIE THEATERS

On Saturdays, the big treat was going to the movies. The offering was a newsreel of current events, seven cartoons, one western serial and a double feature film - all for 12 cents! Hence an entire afternoon was spent in the theater. Even though the price was low, it was sometimes difficult finding the money to attend. With monies tight, we would bring a shopping bag full of popcorn and enjoy the afternoon.

Talk about hustling. In order to buy candy and other treats, I would stand by the aisle entrance and ask people "hey can you spare a penny". Most people obliged. With enough persistence and begging I could scrounge enough money to buy a couple candy bars and really enjoy the show.

Besides buying tickets, there was other methods of egress into the theater. One person would buy a ticket, open the "Emergency "Exit" door and we would sneak in. The money we saved on admission ticket allowed us to buy candy and really enjoy the afternoon. We were successful most times but occasionally got caught. When caught we'd have to buy a ticket for admission. However, the agony of defeat was worth it.

JOBS SUMMARY

As mentioned earlier, I received no allowance and was constantly faced with financial issues at an early age. Therefore, I had to hustle and do odd jobs to make spending money. A summary of some of the jobs I scrounged from an early age until I turned 18 are listed below.

A. 8-12 Years Old

Paper route. At 10 years old, I helped two older boys with delivery of Sunday papers for 50 cents a day. We delivered a whopping 120 papers on a given Sunday! In the summer we used two wagons, in the winter we used two sleds, both with sideboards, respectively, due to the high volume of papers and their damn thickness.

The route netted 5 cents per paper. Tips were fairly common which made for a good payday. My meager share for helping was pretty good considering. The work wasn't all that bad because we sold most of the papers near the Catholic Church after the 8:00, 9:30 and 11:00 Masses. Between masses we made house deliveries in the neighborhood.

After six months the older boys quit and I took over the paper route by myself. Unbeknownst to me the Sunday paper contained many advertisements and features which had to be inserted into the main part of the paper. This sorting alone took almost two hours. Previously the older boys did the sorting so I had no idea of the effort required to insert and sort the papers when I took over.

On the first Sunday of my route, I was so overwhelmed with the sorting procedure (which started around 6:00AM) that I began to cry in despair. That first day my mom helped me and said for me to man up if I wanted to pursue the job. While I later did all the sorting myself, I did get Billy Pett (a very good friend) to help with the deliveries.

Things went pretty smooth with Billy's help at first but I noticed I wasn't making the proper amount of money I should have made for the number of papers delivered. Didn't take long to figure out why. After a couple deliveries I asked Billy to take off both shoes. He hesitated at first but when he did the money shortage was solved. I told Billy to hit the road. From then on, I made all deliveries myself. Quite a job but all the money was mine.

The worst part of the route was collecting money from home delivery customers. Some people left the money under mats, in bottles or paid when I knocked on the door. There were a few shysters who said they would pay next week, etc. but never did owe up. I eventually stopped their deliveries.

On several occasions when I went to collect, they said the money was left by the door. I immediately know what the problem was – Billy. Since he knew my route and which customers left money outside, he helped himself. After a short conversation with Billy with the caveat I would kick his ass if a nickel was missing again, money was never disappeared after that. I then enjoyed this "bump in money" with paper money and tips amounting to about $10 for a Sunday. Not bad for a youngster like me. I subsequently gave up the route after two years.

Mom never asked me for the money I earned on my paper route but I nonetheless I occasionally gave her five dollars each Sunday. I never saved money from delivering my papers. I turned in my paper money around noon. After getting paid, I immediately went next door to hone my skills on pin ball machines. I got pretty adept at playing them but did spend a lot of coins in the process sometimes most of my pay! To this day my pinball skills have not diminished much. I can best my sons all the time on pinball machines – even at my age (82)!

Besides pin ball machines, I had a quicker way of parting with my money. Every Sunday shortly after noontime, the men in my neighborhood met outside of a grocery store (which was closed) for a dice game. Only paper money (i.e., dollar bills) – no coins allowed. Reason for paper money was if the cops came by the money could be quickly scooped up. If I didn't play pinballs, I would rush to the dice game and would donate much if not all of my hard-earned money.

Occasionally, I would break even. However, one Sunday I got hot – I mean really hot! Can't remember how many passes I made but I "broke" the dice game and won over $100 – at 12 years of age! I tried to hide the money from Mom but word got around the neighborhood rather quickly and eventually to Mom. Talked about getting "cleaned out". Mom relieved me of all but $5; she warned me not to play again. Do you think I listened? I played for a while but the eventually group disbanded.

An aside: the cops occasionally came by the money would quickly be scooped up and gambling would stop. They would slow down, stop, sometimes say hello and then leave. Soon after, the game would proceed. It's probably no wonder why the cops didn't disrupt the game - three of our officers were Polish who lived in the neighborhood!

B. 12-15 Years Old

Setting pins in a Bowling Alley.

At an early age I always had an itch to set pins. At that time there were no automatic pin setters. All setting was done manually by an operator (setter) in the pits. This was a prime part-time endeavor as jobs were not plentiful for young kids. In addition, the money was pretty good.

Problem in pin setting jobs was one had to be twelve years of age to set. Reason - in Pennsylvania to be employed setting pins or other work one had to obtain a Work Permit which issued at twelve years of age. I recall sitting in bowling alleys many times and could hardly wait until I turned twelve to get a Work Permit - which I finally did.

I was in the sixth grade when I got my first job setting pins was at the Pulaski Club (Polish Club) bowling alleys. Work started at six in the evening and lasted until 11:00. Worked seven days a week. The money was good but the work was hard. We earned 8 cents per line and usually averaged $12 per week. I usually got home around 11:15 except for occasional distractions.

One distraction occurred when one of our managers would take us to spot light deer after setting pins. The ritual was the manager would buy a quart of beer which he shared with three of us while spotlighting deer – only with lights but no firearms.

Mom never said anything about coming home late as she was usually asleep or at work. She didn't have a problem with staying out late spot lighting deer; however, she knew nothing of the accompanying beer drinking.

Another distraction after setting pins occurred when we occasionally went to a local café which offered all the pancakes one could eat for twenty-five cents. What a treat. I believe the restaurant made no profit feeding us hungry pinsetters because Gene Dolecki had a huge appetite and would scarf 10-12 pancakes at the sitting. Gene he was a big fellow with a size 14 shoe! On these occasions I usually arrived home shortly after midnight with school pending the next day.

The third distraction was stopping by the bakery enroute home. The bakery started preparing goods for the next day late in the evenings. My friends and I would smell the aroma, stop, and buy a loaf of freshly baked bread and butter and scarf it down. Bread was never better then freshly baked.

I mean what the hell was a sixth-grade student doing out till midnight on school nights.

A perk of setting pins was smoking in the "pits". I started smoking and I mean inhaling when I was 12. We were virtuality unnoticeable to bowlers when in the pits. It was an opportunity to puff away unrestricted. Virtually all the pinsetters smoked. Mom never knew of my new found habit. When she smelled smoke on me, I told her it was due to being near smokers. Well, I wished I never started puffing away. This started me on a 26-year smoking career. I did finally quit 44 years ago!

Pepsee was one of the pinsetters – who coincidentally didn't smoke. He had other bad habits. To say he was crafty and creative was an understatement. The alleys had a cashew machine which worked by inserting a nickel in the slot and sliding the lever to the left to release the nuts; the lever would consequently return to its original position ready to receive another coin. In his ingenuity, Pepsee drilled a tiny hole in a nickel and tied a very thin piece of wire to the hole. When the altered nickel was placed in the slot and the lever worked, the altered nickel would trigger the nut discharge and the lever would return to its original position - with the altered coin. In no time were able to empty the machine. The machine was subsequently removed when it was discovered there were no coins in the belly. Now who the hell would have thought of a ruse like this but Pepsee.

Back to setting pins. My uncle Nick ran a 4-lane bowling alley at the YMCA. After a year of setting at the Pulaski Club he asked me to set for him – which I did. Most days we had double leagues. With double leagues you would earn about $3 an evening plus tips. However, there was essentially no break between the leagues. On occasion I set double alleys all night. This was worth about $6.00 each night plus tips. The lanes were closed on Sundays. On a good week I could earn up to $18 – much more than at the Pulaski Club.

All things aside there were several problems setting at the Y. Firstly, the work was very hard and demanding with no breaks. Secondly, there was no smoking in the pits. And thirdly, Uncle Nick was a slave driver. Even though he was my uncle he demanded perfection and treated me as the other setters.

Although I made more money at the Y, I defected after a year setting for Uncle Nick and went back to the Pulaski Club. Uncle Nick was not happy because he knew he lost a hard worker. I never heard the end of it every time I was around Uncle Nick.

Well, all good things must end. The pin setting job only lasted through the fall, winter and spring months. The bowling alleys were closed in the summer because of the heat and lack of air conditioning. I had to find other work for my spending money during the summer.

I worked in the bowling alley setting pins for three years.

C. 15-18 Years Old

Milk Route

My first steady job as a high school sophomore was a milk route with Purity Milk. I inherited the job from a neighborhood friend, Peeker Madden. He was a high school senior and quit the route because of football. I took over his route. The job required delivering milk every other day from 4 AM-until 7 AM - before school hours; in addition, I worked in the plant every other Sunday from 7-12 -after delivering milk all morning. Besides good pay, the beauty of the job was that I needed not work after school hours and had free time to "horse around" while other friends had paper routes or other jobs after school hours.

The milk route routine was as follows: I would wake at 3:30 in the morning. Mom would have breakfast ready I would eat and walk to work. I drove later when I got my driver's license

The work was not easy and demanding since Oil City is hilly and all my customers were on the hilly South Side of town. It was all hustle for three hours with no breaks. It was brutal in the winter time when your hands nearly froze from handling the cold milk – which at that time were all glass bottles. Floyd Southwick, my driver was semi-pleasant to work for. Many times, on the weekends after a night of drinking when I was somewhat sluggish, Floyd would swear at me and occasionally "kick me in the ass" to make me hustle. I didn't blame him as his job was on the line and all complaints fell on his shoulder.

Since the job required a lot of running up and down stairs leading to the heavens, I needed extra nourishment besides my breakfast. Most times I would mix a quart of chocolate milk and a pint of cream for nourishment. Seemed to give me extra energy to complete the route. Also, a good way to clog my arteries. Besides getting money from working the route I was allowed to take home two quarts of milk, a pound of butter, cottage cheese and a pint of cream which Mom loved to use in her coffee.

As mentioned, I worked every other Sunday in the plant from 7:00 AM till noon. Work involved emptying raw milk from the 15-gallon metal containers local farmers brought to the dairy. Later, I ran the machine which washed the glass milk bottles putting them six at a time into the semi-automated moving washer and removing them after the washing. Glass bottles were the word of the day as delivery as paper milk cartons had not yet made the scene.

One pleasant job in the plant was making cottage cheese from curd left over from skim milk production. I would mix curd in a large vessel, add salt and cream to get the desired end product. Of course, tasting the cottage cheese in the process to meet standards was a bonus.

Gas Station Attendant

During the summer of my senior year in high school, and concurrent with my milk route job – yes concurrent to my milk route job - I got a job pumping gas at a very busy cut-rate combination gas station and deli. This job was in addition to the delivery milk job I had from 4AM-7AM. The deli contained meats which I sliced, soda pop and candies (and of course, prophylactics). I sure knew who the guys around town who were scoring.

The job paid $1 per hour which was good wages at the time. The owner was "Porky", a Polish businessman in our neighborhood. He said he hired me because he knew my mom. The job originally was from 8AM until 6PM. It wasn't long before Porky would come by the store and ask me to work late until closing time, which was 10 PM. I didn't mind it because the money was good and jobs were hard to find. Since I had two jobs, I wound up working 7 days a week, alternating between 14 and 18 hours a day - all without a break - as I was the only one running the station. Porky would only show up once a day or not at all to collect the day's receipts.

All told I had only three Sundays off the entire summer! So, with the long station hours and my milk route, I was rich making about $110 per week! Not bad if I say so.

As an another aside, Porky tried to keep track of the gas and food receipts but was not good in his bookkeeping. He pretended to monitor the gas pumped with the cash register sales but soon gave up because the cash register sales did not differentiate or sort gas from deli sales. I thought hell as long as I was working my ass off under slave labor conditions (which no one made me work) I should be entitled to some gas every once in a while. So occasionally sneaking a tank of gas slightly boosted my hourly wage.

Between my milk route and the gas station job, I hardly saw Mom since she worked swing shifts. After work, I would head out for the night and try to stay out of trouble while Mom slept or was working.

In the summer after my freshman year of college I returned to Oil City and got my gas station job back from Porky. The nice thing about it was I had more time to "horse around" because I didn't have the concurrent milk route. Life was good. Summer was good. Good times were even better. After this summer, I only returned to Oil City twice, once for a Christmas vacation and another for a spring break.

The interesting thing about returning to Oil City from college was by car. A 44-hour non-stop trip stopping only to get gas and a burger. My return in the winter was four of us in a 1949 Chevy. We took turns driving. I remember going thru Wyoming and nearly froze to death when my turn in the back seat as heaters were not very efficient in those days.

Odd Jobs
Before the pin setting, milk route and the gas station days, I had numerous odd jobs during my teens with the goal of generating spending cash. There are probably a few I may have omitted but the more notable ones are listed below.

- Mowed yards in the summer. We didn't have power motors back then. All mowing was done by push mowers. I had several customers whose lawns I mowed once a week.
- Speaking of mowing lawns, one summer I worked a couple months mowing grass in a cemetery. The layout was quite hilly and again, we mowed lawns with push movers. The grave sites - 3' X 8' X 6'deep - were dug with shovels by the older workers. However, on one occasion during a manpower shortage, I was recruited to dig a grave site hole. Christ, talk about hard and depressing work that took the cake.
- Painted houses. Some friends got jobs painting houses all summer. They occasionally asked for my help. Five of us could paint a two-story house in about a week. Got ten dollars for my efforts. Ended up helping paint two houses.
- On Saturdays, I cleaned windows of a grocery store for 50 cents. I then walked down the street and swept the floor of a dry-cleaning factory. I got the job because Mom worked with the owner's wife. The sweeping took a good hour to clean the floor. Following this, I cleaned windows in their downtown dry-cleaning store. The two dry cleaning operations netted me $5. All in all, I made $5.50 on a Saturday morning. Not bad for a couple hours work.
- Washed and waxes cars. I had two customers whose cars I would wash and then hand wax once a month each for $5. It was hard work and took several hours to complete each job.
- Helped laundry truck driver with deliveries. Pay wasn't much but I occasionally was allowed to drive the van.
- Occasionally I would help deliver milk from a truck route from my school mate father's farm in the summertime for 25 cents. After deliveries I sometimes got invited to stay at their farm and help with chores such as milking, collecting eggs, etc. Mom allowed me to stay the 2-3 days at a time on the farm.

- One peachy my job was installing car tire chains in the winter. Our town was hilly, so chain requirements were common in the winter. I installed chains on a downtown lot with lot of passing traffic and high visibility. Got one dollar for each job. Sometimes I did six or more installations a snowy day. Good money for little work! Damn hands almost froze off.
- Shoveled snow off driveways and walkways. Hard work which didn't pay much. Hell, I did all kinds of chores for a few pennies. Growing up I always had spending money unlike most of my friends who didn't hustle like I did. I essentially had cornered the neighborhood chore market. If people needed small jobs to be done, they knew who to call.
- I occasionally baby sat two younger boys when I was twelve. The mom once gave me 50 cents to get one son a haircut. Hell, instead I gave him a haircut and kept the money. The mom was not happy with my cutting so I marched him to a barbershop to rectify my butchering job – and relinquish my 50 cents. What goes around comes around.

Liquor Store Job
- I came home for Christmas during my sophomore year in college. As usual, I was looking to make some extra money. The prize job at that time was delivering mail during the holidays. The post office usually hired two part-time workers and paid $2 per hour. Even though my uncle Nick worked at the Post office for many years one of the jobs was awarded to Carl Owens, a good friend of mine whose dad incidentally was the Post Master. No hard feelings I felt happy for Carl. The other job was awarded to someone I didn't know.

As luck would have it, Max Serafin, another Pollack ran the State Liquor Store in Oil City. His daughter, Maxine was in my class. I don't recall how we connected but I got a job unpacking and stacking booze in the display shelves for $2 an hour. I believe him knowing my mom was a factor in procuring the job. Not to my surprise, there were some heavy drinkers in Oil City. Huge amounts of booze went out the door during the short holiday period. I worked in the store for two weeks and headed back to college.

HOPPING TRAINS/PUMPKIN HARVEST TIME

This was not what I consider a job but nonetheless it deserves mention. There were many capers in my early youth which I recollect - some of which I relate – some which I can't. Most of the time Pepsee was a true instigator who cooked up all the schemes.

Railroad train tracks passed near our neighborhood where we often spent time at the depot. Our favorite activity was "hopping trains" - a ride to nowhere and back.

Occasionally, we would hop the trains for a couple miles to our swimming hole up the river. Since they all stopped at a nearby depot, we would usually catch another train on the way home. However, many times we couldn't get a return "hop" and ended up walking home.

Our favorite fall pastime was hopping trains to harvest "free" pumpkins from a large field north of town and sell them. This activity continued thru the fall harvest season but abruptly stopped one day when the farmer stated shooting at us during one of our trips.

I forgot to mention that we actually harvested the pumpkins without paying for them and sold them for a few pennies.

End of pumpkin story.

FLOATING THE RIVER

Another favorite pastime was floating down the river. Pepsee, I, and a couple friends would "hop" a train to Rouseville, a small town a few miles upstream. Oil Creek, which ran thru our city was adjacent to both the railroad tracks and a lumber yard. So, it was convenient for us to hop a train to Rouseville, jump from the train, borrow (steal) planks from the lumber yard, launch them into the creek and float a couple miles down the river to our town. Subsequently we would then sell them for a few pennies to the Goldbergs, our Jewish junk dealers whose yard was adjacent to the creek.

Speaking of Oil Creek and the Goldbergs. We would "snag" suckers and carp fish with bare treble hooks from a railroad bridge that crossed Oil Creek next to the Goldbergs. The creek name was appropriate since the water was highly contaminated with wastes from the Pennzoil and Quaker State refineries upstream. Nobody in their right mind would consider eating fish from the creek – except for our Jewish junk dealers.

There was always competition among us to snag the fish and sell them to the Goldbergs. The suckers were worth ten cents and the larger carp brought twenty cents. It was a win-win for all. The Jews salivated from our fish offerings and we got the money.

SWEET TOOTH

Like everyone else, us kids had a sweet tooth always seeking candies akin to Bill Haley and the Comet's song "Looking in the fish market window like a one-eyed cat". One encounter with sweets involved a distributor warehouse in town that stored cases of candy and other goods. The warehouse foundation was about three feet high made of small bricks. Turns out Pepsee and his friends managed dig out enough bricks to make a hole large enough for one to crawl through. Over a period of a couple weeks, we pilfered the warehouse for boxes of candy like M&Ms, Clark Bars, Mounds bars, etc. – you name it we heisted it.

These forays ended when the warehouse discovered the missing goodies. They also found the hole in the foundation which we entered. They subsequently caught one of us inside the warehouse in the act of pilferage. Other than getting a kick in the ass, we were essentially told not to try it again or they would call the cops. They finally patched up the foundation and we ceased our forays.

In another sweet tooth episode, Pepsee learned that delivery trucks distributing Hostess donuts and other treats parked their unlocked vehicles at night in back of their warehouse. The trucks contained treats left over from deliveries or were loaded for next day deliveries. How he knew about this was beyond me. Anyhow after playing basketball at the "Y", we ransacked the trucks for several nights. The raids stopped after they started locking their trucks at night.

Note to file: Pepsee was a bad influence on me!

FREE FIREWORKS

Another scheme from Pepsee.

Probably one of the most notable and terrified actions I performed in my youth was at about 14 years of age. Pepsee hatched a plan to pilfer fireworks from the Railway Express Station in downtown shortly before the 4th. Railway Express had a delivery/ storage office on the train depot in town. Fireworks at this time were legal and most were shipped by rail because of the bulk of the cartons. You could easily differentiate the fireworks packages from other packages because they had a large diamond-shaped bright red stickers that were clearly marked "FIREWORKS".

The Express depot structure was surrounded by windows on two sides with doors on the two sides. Visibility was clear from either side. The front door side received freight from the train; the opposite side was for customer pickups. The plan was for Pepsee to enter the office from the customer door side and distract the lone inspector on duty. While he was talking to the inspector, I was to enter through the opposite door and grab two boxes of fireworks and hightail it up the railroad tracks. I was very apprehensive and worried and knew if caught it spelled big trouble.

Well, his plan worked. While he distracted the inspector, I entered the back door, grabbed two large boxes of fireworks and ran like hell up the railroad tracks. To say I was scared to death was an exaggeration.

Later, we divided the loot. I hid my share in a storage compartment in my grandmother's house. I had more fireworks than I could ever use. I sold some but discharged most of them with my friends. My mom discovered the fireworks stash. I thought I was in trouble. She asked where I got them. I told her I was holding them for someone for a couple days – and she believed me. I either was one hell of a liar or Mom was highly gullible!

Several firework antics stand out in my mind. In our parochial school lavatory, Simbo, one of my neighborhood schoolmates and myself, on my urging, would both light a cherry bomb, simultaneously throw them in adjacent toilet stalls and immediately flush the toilets. Seconds after the flush the toilets evoked a loud thump as they exploded. We later learned the "thump" damaged the sewage pipes and caused a leak under the concrete. Needless to say, the damage was extensive. Concrete excavation was required to repair the leak. Thank God they never found out the culprit(s). It's a good thing since the nuns warned in school the next day that consequences were dire if they found out who was responsible. Dodged that bullet.

Another firecracker episode involved Pepsee at a Holy Roller Church ceremony. During the service when the congregation was vocalizing and rolling on the floor, we simultaneously launched two cherry bombs (part of our stolen fireworks) into the church. There was a loud boom accompanied by a lot of screaming and hollering. We ran like hell down the street with a couple church members in hot pursuit. Since we knew the neighborhood better than they did, we managed to lose them.

Talk about stupid!

A couple times we lit cherry bombs and threw them into exhaust tail pipes. It was our understanding they did cause some serious damage to exhaust systems.

Stupid times two!

FREE WINTER TIRES

Seems a lot of things were free!

Here's one you probably never heard of. In Western Pennsylvania, especially in our hilly town of Oil City, we received a large amount of snow in the wintertime. Oil City was located in the "Snow Belt" which originated from Lake Erie/Buffalo, extended thru our local Hog Back mountains, and continued on thru the Pittsburg area.

To navigate automobiles in our hilly city, most people had two sets of tires, i.e., "summer tires" and "winter tires". Back in the 50's cars were not equipped with 4-wheel or all-wheel drive so winter tires were required when it snowed - but only on the rear.

In our town, many houses had alleys with a garage behind their homes. Some of these garages were open year around in which people stored one set of their tires. The set stored depended on the weather. Being the entrepreneurs we were, when winter was approaching and snow was forthcoming, we would peruse the alleys at dark and using flashlights shine into the open garages looking for tires - which were usually suspended from the rafters. When tires were spotted, one of us would get dropped off, use a flashlight to identify the size. When we found the size we needed, we would drive around, remove them, throw them the trunk and sneak off into the night. It took a lot of searching and eventually my friend Henry and I were each rewarded with a set of winter tires for our vehicles. I'm sure people were flabbergasted when the season came to change tires and discovered they were missing!

Believe it or not Pepsee was never involved in this charade since he didn't have a car at that time and had no need for tires!

FREE GASOLINE

Even though I usually had spending money, occasionally my funds would get low and I needed to come up with a way to fill up the gas tank. Solution – the "Oklahoma Credit Card" - which consisted of three feet of rubber hose and a five gallon can. It was a risky and somewhat scary endeavor employed in the dark. Getting caught might involve getting your ass kicked or worse turned over to the police.

The hazard was swallowing gasoline at the beginning of the process. After a couple episodes I got the procedure down pat without any swallowing.

One scenario involved siphoning from a large parking lot of the night shift workers at the local steel plant. Another option was driving back roads and looking around farms that had elevated gasoline storage tanks. The farmers usually had long hoses and we'd pull up alongside and fill up. Problem with getting caught here had the consequence that you might get your ass shot. However, the time required to procuring gas by this procedure was a lot less – and less hazardous - than hose siphoning. All in all, it was pretty damn scary business but the gas was free.

The farm siphoning episode ended rather abruptly. After my third attempt, I was driving to town and my car starting sputtering when I reached Oil City. Problem - "White Gas". Autos don't run on the white gas because they don't have the required octane. Of course, my car eventually stopped running. I called Guy. He brought two gallons of gas and towed me into an alleyway. Now I had the problem of emptying the white gas from my tank. I removed the plug on the bottom of the gas tank and drained the tank and let it streak down the alley. The car ran good after pouring in the new gasoline Guy brought me.

Needless, to say my gas siphoning days were finally over. Siphoning gas isn't very prevalent these days because later model cars have anti-theft screens, etc, inside the gas filler tubes. This prevents a hose from getting to the bottom of the tank.

SHOP LIFTING

To say I had sticky fingers was a misnomer. There were three of us bandidos - Benny, Billy and me. Several times a week we would take a couple shopping bags and scour the aisles of Kresseges 5 & 10, Grants Department Store, sporting stores and other businesses. You name it – we lifted it. We lifted playing cards, clothes, games, toys, fishing equipment, etc. Our most prized item was Zippo cigarette lighters. Many folks smoked in those days so it was not hard to sell the lighters for a dollar. We got to a point where we actually took orders before venturing down town to go "shopping".

In our shopping forays we occasionally elicited stares from store employees, especially since one of us usually carried a shopping bag. After a while store employees recognized us, probably suspected what we were up to but couldn't catch us in the act. The ruse worked like this. Two of us would take desired items of merchandise, place them on the counter edge near the aisles and continue on. The "bag man" would follow somewhat behind and quickly throw the material near the edges into the bag without missing a beat.

We were pretty successful and had a good track record - until one day Billy got caught while we were in another part of the store. I remember the police came and scared the crap out of Billy with an admonition that it was juvenile detention if he got caught again. That threat ended our shopping excursions. Probably a good thing.

However, not to underscore the evils of shoplifting there is an old joke that states "When I was a kid you could go to a store with just $1.00 and come home with 4 comic books, 3 candy bars, 2 packs of trading cards, a bag of chips and a cold drink. Now they have cameras everywhere." My how times have changed.

However, shoplifting is still a prevalent issue and out of control. If you wonder why just look at the California law which allows the pilfering of $999 without prosecution. So, it's no wonder the deterrent to stealing in California and many other cities goes unabated.

As an aside to shoplifting, I was offered an opportunity to participate in a lucrative home robbery scheme. It went like this. One day Frenchie showed up on the neighborhood corner where we hung out and pulled out a wad of dollar bills. I mean a big wad of bills. He asked if I'd be interested in getting my hands on this kind of money. He explained how it worked.

He and Simbo worked in pairs. One would go to the front door and distract the occupant which was usually a lady since back in those days men worked and women stayed at home. While one of them was at the front door distracting the occupant the other would enter the house through the back door and rummage thru the kitchen looking for money in cookie jars and other hiding places. In those days many people kept money at home since folks from the old country and others did not have banking or checking accounts. In fact, my grandmother kept her monies in a Bull Durham sack packed away in her bosom.

I don't recall how many houses they pilfered but apparently the ruse was successful. They asked me if I was interested in working with them. While the money was tempting, I believed they crossed the line. Besides getting caught meant juvenile detention. I passed up the opportunity.

Frenchie and Simbo continued the scheme and eventually Frenchie got caught. Don't know how it happened but Frenchie ended "Up the River" in juvenile detention but Simbo was somehow exonerated. In retrospect it was probably the best decision in my life not to participate in their scheme.

WINTER SLEDDING

Winter time provided some interesting opportunities to enjoy the snow. As previously stated, our neighborhood was hilly. During the snow, when cars slowed down on one particular corner to turn and go uphill, we would grab the rear bumper (which they had in the old days) and "hop" a ride. Or vice versa, when coming down the hill to turn the corner, they had to again slow down and we would "hop" a ride. Occasionally we would drop a cherry bomb on the bumper panel and run like hell. Word got out in the neighborhood who was responsible so we quit. We didn't want our asses kicked if we got caught in the act.

On one occasion my cousin Cooper hopped a car and was putting along until he hit a bare spot in the road. He took a summersault and was knocked dizzy. He also got his ass kicked in the process. It was a lose-lose situation for him.

Talk about daredevils. The older kids made a bobsled which had metal runner blades. It held eight people. The run was all downhill for about a quarter mile. It crossed two intersections before it got to the end of the run at the bottom of the hill. Spotters were posted at each intersection and also at the end of the run to watch for cars. Because I was younger, I occasionally got to ride when there was room on the sled.

The design was simple. Wood slats attached to both sides of the sled which acted as brakes. One brakeman on each side. We built up a lot of speed on the way down. It was fun until one time the brakes gave out at the bottom of the hill. We hit a curb, the sled reared up and we were all ejected. Fortunately, there were only minor injuries. Christ it was a wonder no one got killed! Since the sled was badly damaged that ended the bobsled runs.

TEEN AGE DRINKING

If you might surmise from further reading that I drank lot while growing up and also in later college years - you're correct. Proud to say that now I limit myself to a periodic glass of wine or an occasional beer. However, when socializing I do tend to regress somewhat and drink my fair share. Victim of bad habits, I guess.

I started drinking around the age of 12 – mostly at wedding receptions in our community. Receptions were held in two locations in our neighborhood, i.e., Warholics Hall or the Assumption Church Hall. Basically, I was a wedding crasher. I was admitted into the wedding's halls without an invitation mostly because I was "Sophie's Boy". Hell, nobody ever questioned my presence and if they did I 'd say I was related to either the bride or groom.

Food was abundant. Booze flowed freely and was easily available. Early in the wedding festivities I would go to the bar and request a drink. I stated it was for my grandmother, and said she was too tired to get it herself. No problem – most times the pourers were new bartenders who didn't know me – so here's the drink. After the wedding heated up nobody paid attention to "Sophies Boy" drinking. Most times I left the festivities wired.

Weekends in high school spelled beer time. By then I was one of few guys who had a car. I therefore was anointed as the DDD - Designated Drinking Driver.

Heck – there was no problem getting beer at our age. We had several reliable contacts; additionally, one member of our group looked older and, depending on bar and the bartender, was able to buy beer at certain local establishments.

However, our best contact was Paul who lived at K of C Club bar. He was a drinking star and he didn't mind booze trafficking for us. I'd empty my car of passengers, phone Paul and give him my car keys. He would go to the Beer and Ice Shop, put the beer in the drunk and drive my car back to us.

Our favorite beer was a case of Genesee pony bottles (8 ouncers/48 in a case) which we polished off with relish. Our drinking mantra was let's develop a personality; the retort was I'm not too busy.

DRAG RACE DRINKING

One evening after sipping on a case of beer, two carloads of us were heading from Shank's restaurant in Reno to Oil City. At the stop sign and side by side in our cars, Terry Kearney and I decided to have a drag race to Oil City. Shortly after the start of our race, we were pulled over by the State Police and cited for reckless driving which usually had a $50 dollar fine and a six-month suspension of the driver's license.

During the stop, Alex Hahn, who like the rest of us was slightly inebriated, started mouthing off to the officer. We tried to shut him up but he wouldn't keep quiet until he was advised that if he didn't shut up, we'd all be cited for interfering with the law which also carried an additional fine. The officer then advised us that we should expect a registered letter from the State within the next ten days for a court appearance.

Man, my ass was grass! Here I, am counting the days when I would receive my summons to appear in court and pay my fine. Eight days, nine days, ten days and no summons. Back then the deal was if you didn't get a summons within the ten days after the citation, charges were dropped. I was elated since I didn't get the summons within the ten days and I was Scott free!

At the time I didn't know why no summons arrived. Found out later that Terry Kearney's dad was an alderman, sort of a local judge, who put in a word for us and had the charges dismissed. Man, I must live a charmed life!

KEG PARTIES

The initial keg gathering occurred toward the end of my senior year of high school. The party was to be held in Sam Brown's parents' cottage in the resort of Henrys Bend, about 6 miles from town. The school was abuzz about the party and about thirty guys were in attendance which included mostly seniors and some underclassmen. Don't remember how we got the beer but it was a 2-kegger.

The party was in full swing until two Sherriff cruisers came upon the scene with their gumball machines in full color. Unbeknownst to us word also got around to Maggie Boll, our English teacher, that the party was on. Apparently, she warned the law about the event. She bared us out probably because she was upset and didn't get an invite. Nonetheless, the Sheriff showed up. Sam went to greet them. They wanted to know who owned the property and yada-yada-yada. Eventually most of us went outside to get in on the conversation. After explaining to the Sheriff who owned the property and what the event was the Sheriff said things were cool as long as we weren't causing damage or bothering neighbors. They left convinced things were under control – which believe or not they were. Us drunks never fought with another.

Following graduation summer keg parties were the rage. Guy and I were in charge of the affairs. We would both collect a dollar anyone who might be interested. Guy made arrangements to procure the keg. Kegs then cost $16. We were familiar with boys of interest and had no problem getting the $16 – we usually collected more than needed.

Initially we charged $1.25 and thereby were able to buy a tap which I kept for future use; subsequently we then only charged a dollar a head. I might mention that it was a boy only affair and we had them every about every two weeks. Locations were not advertised until the date neared. We chose different places for these events usually in wooded areas or places of relatively safety to evade the law. We had a contact who was old enough to buy the keg so we didn't pay any buyer fees.

Five of these gatherings went smoothly – no fights, etc. considering the atmosphere. The law got wind of these gatherings and wanted to put a stop to them. On the fifth gathering someone shouted "cops" and everyone scattered. The law was pretty damn slow and didn't catch anyone but they did confiscate the keg and our tap. They also got wind of who sponsored the gathering but didn't know the buyer.

The last gathering happened two weeks before I was bound to college. Word got out that the cops wished to interview Guy and me. For whatever reason my interview never happened since I left town. I later learned from Guy that they did talk to him but he offered them no info and they never found out who bought the kegs.

WEEKEND DRINKING

In high school we looked forward to the weekend that exclusively involved beer drinking, going to Friday and Saturday night dances at the YMCA and YWCA. In the summer, dances were also held on Wednesdays at the YMCA. Oil City had no corners where gangs hung out so we had no turf battles. Basically, our group and other groups were out for a good time drinking and riding around town.

Even though we were a friendly group we occasionally got into skirmishes with out-of-towners – usually at the dances – over girls. There were more or less four groups of us. We all knew each other. We never fought with each other. It's like there was honor among thieves. Our mantra was "Let's drink up a personality".

For all the drinking our group did on the weekends we were never stopped by the local police. I believe we were astute enough not to get caught since I know the local fuzz would have gotten great enjoyment from hauling us in.

There was, however, an older group of high school guys who were bad hombres when drinking. In contrast to our friendly groups, they were mean dudes. The group included Gunzy, Peeker, Chops and Nuts - all football players and all temperamental dudes when under the influence. They were tri-city terrors constantly involved in altercations. In one episode, they initially got into a shouting match with "Bear Weaver" and his group which also hung out by the "Y". Then all hell broke loose. Things escalated into a rumble and the cops were called to calm things down. Didn't happen. The two cops who arrived on the scene tried to restore order but were outmanned. They called for reinforcements. Eventually it took six law enforcement officers to subdue them and run them in. Like I said, they were mean hombres.

AUTOMOBILE HISTORY

I couldn't find an appropriate chronological section in this book to insert my auto history so I thought this might be an appropriate place to do so. I include this history as it exemplifies some of the twists and turns that never seemed to stop.

1934 PLYMOUTH

The driving age in Pennsylvania was 16 years old. I bought my first car when I was 15 ½ years of age.

During the summer of 1956, I worked for Mr. Busko, a carpenter who was building a house. I worked 8 hours a day from Monday thru Friday and four hours on Saturday. Much of the work was outside. The worst was digging a trench for the underground sewage pipes from the house to the street. The ground was heavy clay and progress was slow and hard.

Once the outdoor work was complete, I started working indoors. My best experience was installing an oak floor with tongue and groove slats. Another great experience was installing and lining the many closet walls with cedar strips.

At that time the minimum wage was 75 cents per hour. Mr. Busko, an immigrant Polish-speaking tightwad, paid me 50 cents per hour. I never complained because jobs were hard to find and besides, I was making $22/week – a small fortune and good money for that time. Looking back, I should have taken court action against Mr.

Busko to recover the 25 cents/hour that I was entitled to. When I found out I had recourse to recover my back wages, I confronted Mr. Busko and advised I was going to sue him for the money he owed me in back wages for my work with him. However, after several discussions he agreed to pay me $30 for my lost wages. Great win!

Finally, I had enough had enough money to buy a car. I had my eye on a 1934 Plymouth with a rumble seat owned by Buckwheat. He would drive the vehicle up and down the hill past the corner where we hung out. One day out of the blue I asked him if he would sell his car. He said if I had $75 the car was mine. Sold! The problem was that I wasn't yet 16 and could not legally drive. I needed but didn't have a drive permit or a license. While that was a huge impediment it did not stop me from driving around the neighborhood. I was in heaven! I drove the car around the neighborhood for several weeks to the envy of my friends since out of the 10-12 guys who hung around the corner, George Monks was the only one who had a car – a 1937 Chrysler.

As an aside, I never told my mom about buying the Plymouth. I stored the vehicle in a neighbor's garage. He did not charge me anything because I mowed his lawn, washed his car and occasionally watched his two boys.

However, the fun of driving around the neighborhood came to an abrupt end. As I came around a corner on a blind turn, I ran into a later model Plymouth owned by Mayor Mike, the most hated guy in our neighborhood. Mayor Mike was in his late forties, smoked cigars and didn't like kids even though he had two of them. The accident wasn't really my fault because Mayor Mike was in the middle half of my lane when I hit him. Nonetheless, he said he was going to call the police and report the accident. I begged him not to but he stood firm. Turns out Mayor Mike's brother was my uncle Nick, who coincidentally was not overly fond of his brother. I hurriedly boogied up to my uncle Nick's house which was a half block away, told him the story and asked if he could talk to his brother not to call the cops. Mayor Mike relented and agreed not to call the fuzz if I paid for his damage even though he agreed the accident was not my fault. It was agreed I would to pay for the damage and he would not call the cops. I didn't tell my mom about the accident. However, she soon found out when word got out around the neighborhood. To my surprise the only thing she said was that's what you get for breaking the law – she never said anything about my purchase of the car.

Shortly after the accident my car had a carburetor problem and stopped running. Because of the accident with Mayor Mike I had no money to fix the problem so I sold the car for $50.

1948 FORD

I then bought a 1948 Ford for $100 with help from my mom. I agreed to pay her $10 a month to pay off the money she loaned me to buy the car. What a pig the Ford was. Seems like I was always having issues with it. So, I sold it for junk after I paid off my mom.

1953 CHEVROLET

I then coerced my mom to loan monies so I could buy a two-tone green 1953 Chevy with the caveat that I teach her to drive and pay her $15 a month – both of which I did. A win-win for both of us. My portion of the payments were made as agreed but her driving lessons did not happen. After two practice drives, one in which we almost bought the farm, I gave up and told her I would find someone to instruct her how to drive.

As I previously mentioned, my mom worked at a glass plant making bottles located next to Koppers, a chemical manufacturing plant. Turns out the plant had an explosion which spewed chemicals in the air and some which landed on the parked cars in the glass plant parking lot. My mom's car was one the vehicles which pitted the cars paint job. Koppers agreed to paint all autos affected by the spill – which included mom's car.

At the time the rage among my high school driving friends was customized cars with funky paint jobs. Bob McKinley had a 1954 Olds painted light purple; Bob Hovis 1953 Ford - candy apple red; Jim Fox 1951 Chevy – peach, Guy's 1953 Pontiac - bright blue, etc. Me - I had mine pained Tropic Turquoise. These were high visible cars that were paraded around Main Street on the weekends. Talk about recognition, everyone knew who we were – including the local police.

However, my luck with the new paint job took a funny twist. After finishing free the paint job Mr. Allen told me the hood was not secure since the lock was taken off when I customized the car and was only secure by wires. He told me to drive carefully until I reattached the hood lock. Going down the hill as I drove away from the auto painting shop the damn wire securing the hood broke and the hood flipped up obscuring my vision. I was able to safely stop the vehicle at the side of the road. Unfortunately, sprung hood had damaged the newly painted portions of the front fender.

I returned the damaged car to Mr. Allen. He banged out the dents, repainted the damaged sections and reinstalled the hood lock - all at no charge. I was in business. I drove the car until the fall of 1958 and left the car to my mom when I went to college. Funny thing was that when folks saw mom driving the "car" they asked where's Mincer. So, the legacy of my car lived on. Years later mom sold the car and bought a used Buick.

1949 CHEVROLET

I had no vehicle in college until the summer of my senior year. Talk about a bummer. I broke dates because I had no wheels. I promised to wash or wax cars and thank God occasionally a frat brother would loan me his car.

When college started in my senior year, I buckled down on my studies and had no time for dates. However, my friend Dave had many dates and a car but had an accident which put him without wheels. So, what does Dave do? Well, he calls on his friend Frank for help. The conversation went like this: Dave would call and ask Frank how are you doing? At first, I said doin' okay since I was busy studying, this then followed with "Er... do you think I could borrow your car this evening? Sure Dave. After several rentals Dave would call and before he could say anything I said yes, Dave, you can borrow my car. While Dave was my best friend, he had a habit of not putting gas in my car. Since Dave and I were always broke hombres, I never asked him to gas it up. What the hell are friends for anyway?

1956 CHEVROLET

I left Utah State and headed to Corvallis, Oregon to do graduate work at Oregon State. Shortly after I arrived, the drive shaft on the damn 1949 Chevy locked up and was undrivable. The repair itself was not difficult but I didn't know much about car repairs. However, the repair cost was pretty high. In fact, the price of a used car was somewhat comparable to the repair costs. I looked around but was unable to immediately find a low-priced used auto. I finally found and bought a 1956 Chevy - a bit higher than I anticipated but turned out to be a great vehicle. I had it for six years and sold it for $75 when I went to Boston. Wish I still had it.

1970 FORD STATION WAGON

Prior to leaving Boston and heading to my first post college job in California, we celebrated by purchasing a new station wagon. On driving out of the dealer's lot, I noticed thick blue smoke coming out of the tail pipe. I made a U-turn and headed back to the dealership. They diagnosed a valve problem and repaired it.

At this time, my son Michael, was two weeks old. The plan heading to California was to stop in Havana, Illinois, Patty's home town, to show off the baby to her folks. It was decided Patty would fly to Chicago and I would drive with me and our dog and hookup in Havana and spend a week there.

I made it to Havana but a day later my transmission went out. Fortunately, it was repaired before departing to California. Again, the plan was for me to drive to California and Patty would fly to San Francisco and stay with her sister in San Rafael. I would meet her there and look for a place in Richmond near my new job.

And guess what - I drove the wagon for seven years without any incident. It was the best vehicles I ever owned.

JAMESTOWN, NEW YORK

It may sound like we drank a lot – and we did but only on weekends. Word got around that there were two bars in Jamestown, New York that served under age youths. Jamestown was only an hour across the border from Oil City about an hour's, drive.

At that time, the drinking age in Pennsylvania was 21. The drinking age in New York was eighteen. So, it didn't take a rocket scientist for us to figure out New York here we come. The potential and excitement to snuggle up to a bar and get served was intoxicating in itself.

In order to get served in New York, a driver's license or a "Draft Card" were acceptable forms of identification. Draft cards were the way to go. In the 50's male youths who reached 18 were required by law to register for the draft and were subsequently issued a "Draft Card". The "Draft Card" had no photo and only listed a date of birth.

One particular bar in Jamestown was known to serving youths under 18. Word got around that the bar didn't require identification to get served. However, in the event identification was required we came prepared. We would borrow a "Card" from a friend and use that for identification since no photo was present to connect the holder to the photo. Most times all of us (usually four) could procure a Card to use. However, on one particular occasion one of us had no "Card". So, when we snuggled up to the bar the first person would pass his card underneath to the last seated person who had no card and show it to the bartender thereby allowing all of us to get served. This place was so popular with kids in Oil City that on one occasion we met another car load of our friends, unbeknownst to each group that either was heading to Jamestown that night.

We took to backroads in returning to Oil City to lessen our chances to be pulled over. These were usually two-lane winding country roads on one of these trips we were returning at night at an elevated rate of speed past H&H Farms. Out of nowhere two horses appeared in the middle of the road. We veered and luckily avoided hitting them. However, we found out later that another car behind us wasn't fortunate and died after hitting the horses. You might call that biting the bullet!

As usual, all good things must come to an end. Our particularly ending occurred when on a visit to our frequented Jamestown bar there was patron who was somewhat loud and heavily tattooed. He said something to our Bill Courtney, the largest (and toughest) kid in our foursome. One thing led to another and exploded when Butch Quinn asked the tatted guy if he worked in the circus side show. The guy took offense, got in our faces and offered to go outside but somehow an altercation between Courtney and the tatted guy erupted inside the bar. Courtney quickly ended the discussion; however, we quickly left after the bartender called the cops. After that, we never made any more trips to Jamestown. Now with our Jamestown connection was over, beer procurement options now depended on local contacts.

As an aside, a Jamestown tragedy did occur. One foursome car load Oil City young men, which had as a passenger a neighborhood kid we hung out with, weren't as fortunate. Evidently traveling at a high rate of speed they were unable to negotiate a curve, ran off the road and sheared off a telephone pole. Our friend, and two other passengers was killed; only the driver survived.

A PROM NIGHT TO FORGET

A disastrous drinking night to say the least – not because I had a date but because I didn't. You couldn't write a script for what transpired this night. I had no date to our Junior Prom; neither did Jerry Lee, Carl and Les. We loaded up my car with two cases of ponies (48 bottles which we obtained thru our loyal contact and headed late afternoon to Titusville, (about 8 miles from Oil City) because Carl wanted to see a girl friend of his. She rounded up three other friends and we took of riding in her dad's new car. By this time the beer kicked in and we were feeling our oats. Carl was a bit frisky and somehow his footprints appeared on the roof liner and left several shoe marks. Finally, after getting obnoxious and unruly, the girls dumped us off and told us to get lost.

By this time, it was dark and we headed back to Oil City. There was a Drive-In-Theater midway between the Oil City and Titusville. For whatever reason Carl said it would be nice if he had rear seat speakers in his car. No problem. We entered the drive-in thru the exit, parked in several empty spaces and subsequently tore out four speakers – two for me and two for Carl - from the posts and headed back out the exit. I installed two of the speakers in the back of my car - low-cost stereo.

Back in Oil City in the evening things just started to heat up. We drove around town with windows down whooping and hollering. It's a wonder we weren't stopped by the cops. In one instance we came to a construction site that had small round kerosene lamps burning to highlight the site. We grabbed three of them and held one out each window as we drove through town, eventually throwing them from the car. One rolled under a car while lit – but hey, we weren't about to stop and kept going. Apparently as we later learned, some minor damage occurred to the paint job.

Next, we headed up to Hasson Heights (an upscale development) and proceeded to do figure eights on several lawns tearing up the grass. In this development the mail boxes were situated on the lawns next to the street. On someone's urging, I straddled the street/lawns and mowed down six mailboxes in the process. Caveat: the next day I noticed large scratches on my bumper and clumps of grass around the underside and outside of my car.

Our final highlight of the evening was getting rid of empties. On leaving the Hasson Heights area, we drove through Hasson Park about 3:00AM. By then we had consumed the two cases of beer. As we snaked thru the winding road of the park, we smashed all the empty bottles on the roadway. Man, we were drunk.

Following the park episode, I dropped Carl and Les off in their neighborhoods on the South Side of town. They apparently weren't done for the night. They threw bird baths and other decorative lawn items onto the street breaking them. Someone called the cops and the chase was on. They successfully evaded the police but not before they had done considerable damage.

The morning newspaper had a lengthy and descriptive narrative of the damage caused the night before by vandals. That morning I went to see Jerry Lee. As were sitting at the table and his dad was reading the newspaper he asked if we heard about the vandalism reported in the paper. Of course, we said no but he had a smirk on his face and seemed to know that Jerry & I might have been somehow involved. While none of us fessed up about our exploits somewhat the word got out. Events such as this in our town were quickly disseminated thru the town's underground Western Union. Whether good or bad everyone in town new within hours who were the perpetrators. No secrets were sacred in town. I guess most small towns are like that.

JAIL TIMES

Drinking exploits would not be complete without a description of several tri-city incidents.

A. Oil City

Three of us were picked up for driving and underage drinking and escorted to the police station. We were quizzed on who provided the beer. They gave us the third degree and scared the hell out of us saying we faced jail time if we didn't identify our source. Jim Stabler who was the car driver at the time of the arrest spilled the beans. He said we got it from Bobbie Morrison. Under threat of an overnight stay, Jim was allowed to call his older brother, a lawyer, who got us out of spending the night in jail. However, we were told there were to be consequences for driving and underage drinking.

Time went on and we never heard any more about the booze, jail, etc. Reason: Bobbie's dad was the fire chief; local politics at work.

In addition to being detained by the police for drinking under age, several of us were guests of the department for gambling on the street corner. It was common for us to have poker games on the sidewalk of a four-car intersection. Swearing and other noises were common especially by the losers.

The poker crowd usually numbered six to ten people. Residents in one of the corner houses constantly complained about the noise. Since we were not on private property, they couldn't disperse us - until two police patrol cars arrived. We thought nothing of it since we knew all the police and they had passed us many times when games were in progress. Nonetheless they stopped, piled us into two cruisers and hauled eight us off to jail.

Big mistake! They put all eight of us into one jail cell. Problem. The noise level in the cell increased, with cat calls and all. Guys were doing chin ups on the pipes and banging on the jail bars. We were told to shut up but we didn't. The problem facing us was our parents needed to appear to release us from jail. My mom was working. So, my aunt, cousin Frankie's mom, bailed both of us out. All in all, it was a chicken shit maneuver by the police. In the long run it was no deterrence as we continued to play poker on the street corner and quickly pick up money when we saw the police coming.

The police must have not had bigger fish to fry in lieu of harassing us.

B. Titusville

This event was quite serious and involved an overnight stay in the caboose. As was the case on many nights, Bill Courtney, one of our group, could get served in local bars and get beer to go - even though he was only 18 like the rest of us. As was usual custom, we would drive around town drinking. One evening – Guy decided and I don't know the exact reason – we ended up drinking on a Thursday night, not a normal drinking night. We ended up in Titusville, a town 8 miles from Oil City, which we frequently visited.

Around eleven in the evening we were riding around and Guy discovered we were almost out of gas. Problem was we had no money between us to buy gas. Courtney said no problem. He said to find someone walking on the street and I will "roll" him for some money. Well, he did and extricated two dollars from the man. While we headed for a gas station, the rolled victim hailed down a cop cruiser and told the police what occurred. It didn't take long to find Guy in his bright blue Packard. Guy tried to out run the cops but they cornered us in an alley.

The cops piled us into the cruiser for a night in the caboose. Several snags. One: they would not let us out of jail until our parents appeared. Two: Guy had to drive to Pittsburg at 4:00 AM to pick up wholesale groceries for their fruit business. Three: I was to report to my gas station work at 8:00 in the morning. Fourth: we couldn't get released until the next morning.

Meanwhile, then shit hit the fan. To this day, I believe the police regretted keeping overnight. While incarcerated, we raised hell all night in the jail, singing, hollering, requesting a phone call – which they denied until the next morning, demanded they provide us with food – which they also denied. The caveat was no release unless an adult bailed us out in the morning.

The next morning Guy's dad appeared early. He wasn't very happy, but somehow was able to get all of us released. Surprisingly, no charges were filed against any of us for the theft and fleeing from the police.

Guy got his ass chewed out by his dad. I almost lost my gas station job because Porky had to get his fat ass up to open the gas station. He wasn't too pleased. When I showed up later for work and he let me know how pissed he was in so many words! Bill Courtney and Norman Quinn had no jobs and didn't need to report for work.

Mom asked me where I spent the night. I told her I stayed at Guy's and didn't come home because it was too late. She believed me. To this day she never knew what happened.

Wow - sweated out another bullet!

C. Franklin

Oil City, Titusville and Franklin were a tri-city area 8-10 miles apart with Oil City in the middle. It wasn't my goal or intention to be incarcerated in all three cities but it did happen.

Guy and I went on a drinking spree and again for whatever reason he wanted to go to a semi-upscale Franklin bar/restaurant to have a drink. Tony Giardano, the owner, was from Oil City. He knew Guy. He was not a fan of Guy and vice versa. Guy had previous issues with him in a nightclub he previously owned in Oil City.

We tried to enter the premises but were denied admission for lack of proper attire. Guy and I got into a scuffle with the doorman and Tony called the police. We were hauled in for disturbing the peace. The problem again was for Guy since he had to make an early morning produce run to Pittsburgh. In order to be released we had to have someone come to jail to bail us out. The last thing Guy wanted was to wake his dad again. As it turned out Guy had an uncle in Franklin who likewise had a produce business. Guy called him and he bailed us out.

Thank God- -no overnight jail time!

FOREST RANGER

Change of subject.

Late in my senior year of high school I wondered what I might do after graduation. I had a part-time job delivering milk. The dairy I worked at offered me a full-time job after graduation as a truck driver with my own route. The pay was $80 a week with incentive bonus for procuring new customers. Sounded like a pretty good job at that time since I believe I could procure several new customers in our neighborhood for the accompanying bonus. I considered taking the job. However, I truly liked the outdoors and wanted to be a forest ranger.

Upon contacting the Pennsylvania Game Commission, I was advised that a college education was required. Who the hell said one needed a degree to become a Forest Ranger.

So, late in my senior year of high school I applied to schools that had forestry curricula. They included Syracuse, Penn State, Ohio State and Duke. Much to my dismay, they all rejected my application for admission. Perhaps it was because of my high school grades. A look at my senior of high school report card (Figure 5, shown below), confirmed why I wasn't academically acceptable. Hell, no wonder I was denied admissions.

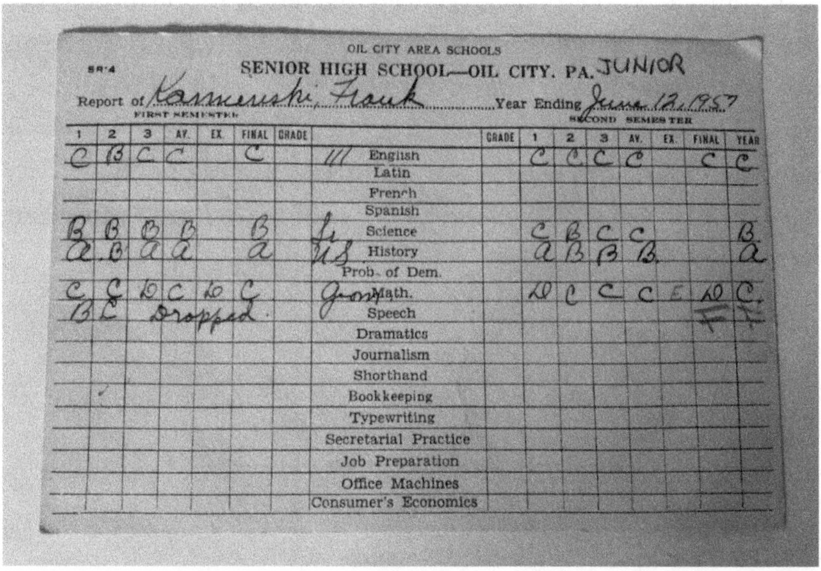

OIL CITY AREA SCHOOLS

SR-4 SENIOR HIGH SCHOOL—OIL CITY, PA. JUNIOR

Report of Kamienski, Frank Year Ending June 12, 1957

1	2	3	AV.	EX.	FINAL	GRADE	FIRST SEMESTER / SECOND SEMESTER	GRADE	1	2	3	AV.	EX.	FINAL	YEAR
C	B	C	C		C		III English		C	C	C	C		C	C
							Latin								
							French								
							Spanish								
B	B	B	B		B		Li Science		C	B	C	C			B
a	B	a	a		a		US History		a	B	B	B			a
							Prob. of Dem.								
C	C	D	C	D	C		Geom Math.		D	C	C	C	E	D	C
B	C	Dropped					Speech							F	F
							Dramatics								
							Journalism								
							Shorthand								
							Bookkeeping								
							Typewriting								
							Secretarial Practice								
							Job Preparation								
							Office Machines								
							Consumer's Economics								

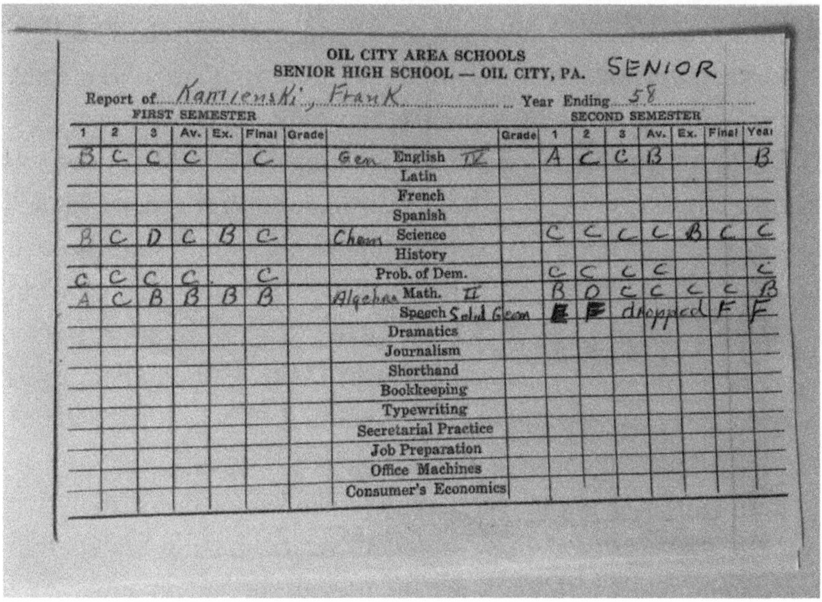

OIL CITY AREA SCHOOLS

SENIOR HIGH SCHOOL — OIL CITY, PA. SENIOR

Report of Kamienski, Frank Year Ending 58

1	2	3	Av.	Ex.	Final	Grade	FIRST SEMESTER / SECOND SEMESTER	Grade	1	2	3	Av.	Ex.	Final	Year
B	C	C	C		C		Gen English IV		A	C	C	B			B
							Latin								
							French								
							Spanish								
B	C	D	C	B	C		Chem Science		C	C	C	C	B	C	C
							History								
C	C	C	C		C		Prob. of Dem.		C	C	C	C			C
A	C	B	B	B	B		Algebra Math. II		B	D	C	C	C	C	B
							Speech Solid Geom		E	F	dropped			F	F
							Dramatics								
							Journalism								
							Shorthand								
							Bookkeeping								
							Typewriting								
							Secretarial Practice								
							Job Preparation								
							Office Machines								
							Consumer's Economics								

Figure 5

Not to be deterred, I subsequently applied to Colorado State, University of Colorado and Utah State. I was accepted at Colorado State and Utah State. I chose Utah State since their out-of-state tuition was only $100 per quarter compared to $300 per quarter at Colorado State.

SAT scores were not in play in the late 50's, and admission criteria for some colleges were rather loose. As described below, my college admission experience was probably very different from today's requirements.

My college experiences are outlined below.

UTAH STATE 1958-1962

My only stipulation for admission into Utah State was to take a written entrance exam. The exam was used as a yard stick to measure academic skills. Apparently, I didn't fail the exam but was required to take "bonehead" English to bring my communication skills up to university standards.

A. Housing

I never traveled more than fifty miles from Oil City. My only option to Utah State was a plane ride to Salt Lake City. I had never flown in an airplane before. The thought of airplane ride was apprehensive. Nonetheless, I arrived in the Salt Lake City airport around 6:00 PM.

The immediate burning issue was housing. I had no idea where I would be living upon my arrival. Normally incoming freshmen were required to live in university dorms. I was advised that because of my late application the dorms were full. The only housing references I had was a university listing of potential housing with addresses and telephone numbers.

I called a few places in Logan for lodging. I finally hooked up with a rooming house that accepted students and told the lady to hold a place for me. I then took a bus from the airport to Logan, which was about an hour from Salt Lake. I arrived late in the evening and took a cab to my housing destination. It was an approved off-campus house with separate rooms for boarders. While there I met Joe Delgado from Pocatello who was also rooming there. He had arrived earlier in the day. We became instant friends.

The house was old. The rooms were small. The food was iffy. The third morning, the host/owner, a lady, asked if we wanted bacon and French Toast. Yes! Well, the toast was fried in the bacon grease! After this and other awful breakfasts, Joe and I looked at each other and decided we needed to find new housing.

Neither of us had a vehicle. We walked a couple miles up to campus and headed to Student Housing to find alternate digs. We had no idea where the Housing Office was and asked the first person we saw where the Office was located. As it turns out the guy we asked for directions was "Corky" Jones from Salt Lake who belonged to the Sigma Nu Fraternity. He asked us if we were looking for a place to live. We said yes. He said he belonged to a fraternity and they have a newly built house which was not full and they were looking for bodies to fill it.

Well, it turns out, we were welcomed to room at the frat house. We only had to pay room and board. We were assigned to a 6-man dorm. Food was very good. Maude was a great cook! Two meals a day were served five days a week, no meals on Saturday and one meal on Sunday. Better than living in dorms and eating dreadful cafeteria food. Talk about falling into a cesspool and coming out smelling like a rose.

All through college I never had much spending money. I was literally broke after paying room and board, admission fees, and buying books and school supplies. Since the last meal of the week was on Friday and the next one was noon on Sunday, I had to forage for myself on Saturdays. There were several Saturdays when I had no money to even buy a hamburger. I didn't really know anyone who could lend me money and my roommate Joe headed to Pocatello almost every weekend. So, on several occasions, I went a day and a half without any food. Life was rough so was my empty stomach.

B. Freshman Year

Needless to say, I didn't fare academically well in my first quarter. Not familiar with the university policy to quit (drop) a class was the requirement to get the instructor's signature and formally drop the class with the Registrar. There were two such occasions where I failed to do so and got an "F" – one in freshman football and the other in Forest Management, my major.

When I went for football tryouts, they asked what position I wanted to play. Possessing some athletic abilities (at least in my mind) I said quarterback would be the ideal spot for me. They asked about my football experience. I said I never played in high school but played a lot of sand lot football. After the two practices, reality set in. I was 5'10" and weighed about 150 lbs. When I was tackled by brutes 200+ lbs. I quickly decided football would do me better as a spectator sport so I quit. As outlined above, I got an "F" grade in freshman football.

So, to pursue my endeavor to become a Forest Ranger, I was required to take a Forestry Management course. Besides being boring, the instructor, a well-recognized scientist in his field, was rather uninspiring. So, after several lectures, I quit going to class. My second "F" in my first quarter of college. One might surmise that my academic performance was a train wreck based on my first quarter performance.

In the second quarter of my freshman year, I was awarded an "F" in botany, a major course which negatively impacted my grade point. Subsequent to this lack luster academic performance, I received a letter from the Dean specifying I was on probation. If I didn't maintain a "C" average next quarter, I would be awarded a "Rhodes Scholarship", i.e., shape up or "Hit the Road". Talk about a wake-up call. Well in the final quarter of my freshman year with doomsday hanging over me, I barely did manage a C+ average and was allowed to continue my studies into my sophomore year. Coincidentally, the next quarter I got an "A" in my botany class! Talk about a 180!

C. Sophomore Year

The academic problem in my freshman year was I didn't know how to study since I never did in high school. However, in my sophomore year I somewhat buckled down. I became interested in insects and changed my major to Entomology. I also became interested in chemistry, the result of having a wonderful instructor who took the fog out of the introductory chem class.

D. Junior/Senior Years

My junior and senior years were more productive. There were three academic achievements I was very proud of. The first was Human Physiology. The test consisted of 50 true or false questions. I got all answers correct. Dr. Baylor announced to the class of about 100 students that I was the only to ever answer all questions correctly. Two other achievements - one was a grade of 100 in an Organic Chemistry which Dr. Olsen stated only occurred twice in his classes. The third achievement was an A in Human Genetics – one of the few A's Dr. Gardner issued in his class. You might say I now was a serious student.

I studied very hard in my senior year. The benefit of my toils were Fellowships offers from University of Kansas, Kansas State, Oregon State and University of Wisconsin to do graduate work. I chose Oregon State for two reasons: (1) I worked there a month in the summer and (2) their graduate program offered an opportunity in insect biochemistry research, my prime interest.

Lack of finances almost ended my academic career. I didn't have enough money to make it through my senior year living in the frat house. Richard Brumley, one of my fraternity brothers from Logan, said I could live with his parents paying only $30 a month for room and board. I took their offer and moved in. Two months later I literally ran out of money. I had a very difficult course schedule which precluded me from part time employment. The Brumleys allowed me to stay until the end of my senior year without any payments. Wow – what a tremendous break! To this day I am indebted to them and never forgot their great generosity. Incidentally, I later repaid them for the last seven months of living there.

COLLEGE JOBS

Since I was perpetually broke during my undergraduate years, I performed any job that paid a few bucks. A chronology of these jobs is listed below.

FISH & WILD LIFE CHECK STATION

In my freshman year shortly after getting settled in, I saw an ad for deer checking with the Utah Department of Fish & Wildlife at the Utah/Colorado border. It involved a weekend of monitoring a checkpoint in 8-hour shifts. The pay was fairly good for the work we performed. This job only lasted for three weekends.

FRAT HOUSE MEALS

Meals at the frat house required that three brothers served, bused and cleaned pots and pans for a full week on a rotating basis. It took about an hour or so to finish the chores. This meant your number was called only once every 4-5 weeks. However, older brothers, especially those on the G.I. bill, were rather lazy and gave one dollar for each day that someone substituted for them. I usually took their turn one or two times a month for the extra money.

FIGHTING FOREST FIRES

Following the summer of my sophomore, I worked as a fire fighter in the Boise National Forest. There were 7 in our crew – four from Utah State, one from University of Georgia, a local from Boise and our leader from Iowa. Idle times around camp were fun, i. e. painting fences, fishing in a local stream. Best part was coon and bobcat hunting with three dogs the Boise guy had in camp.

We were required and paid for 5 days in camp. We were on fire call half a day on Saturday and generally off on Sundays – unless there was a callup for a fire. In those instances, and depending on the severity of the fire, we were away from camp anywhere from 1-2 days. On overnight stays we slept on the ground in sleeping bags we packed in our van.

We were once called up on a project fire – a serious fire that was labeled as a Crown Fire meaning the fire was spreading from treetop to treetop. Our tenure on one such fire lasted 10 days. On project fires when we were constantly on the fire line the only equipment, we had were a back pack, shovel or a Pulaski, a canteen of water and "C" rations.

Since we were mobile and constantly on the move, we had no sleeping bags. We subsequently made beds from a dug depression lined with pine needles and covered ourselves with pine limbs to keep warm. Daylight temperatures were usually in the 90's but dipped down to the 30's at night. To say the least, life was miserable at night.

Occasionally, on a lightning fire from a smoldering tree on or two of us – depending on the severity of the fire were helicoptered in to douse the embers and subsequently be picked up when the fire was secured. On one occasion, one of our crew was helicoptered on a snag fire. Shortly after being dropped off, he was stung by a scorpion and had a reaction to the venom and had difficulty breathing. He was picked up two days later by a chopper and transported to a hospital where he remained in intensive care treatment for five days.

I myself once ended up in the hospital for a couple days to pluck slivers from my belly after sliding down a telephone while replacing wire. The spikes attached to my boots which were used to shimmy up the pole hit a soft spot and I slid down the pole with my stomach touching the pole on my way down. Fortunately, I had gloves on so no slivers entered my hand. It was a painful experience.

On the Sundays we had off, we would head into Boise and go honky-tonking Saturday night and buy groceries the next day.

Problem with the weekend forays we had no place to sleep during the night. Several times we would unroll our sleeping bags and crash on a nearby lawn.

One morning while "Lawn camping", we crashed in a city park for the night. During the night I was awaken by somebody kicking me in my sleeping bag and telling me to "get up. After a profanity laced response, I looked up to see two Boise policemen who reiterated their greeting and told to us get out of Dodge – which we quickly did. We did continue to come to town on permitted weekends but were never bothered by the law.

BEE HIVE TRANSFERS

In my junior year, I switched my major from Forestry to Entomology. Turns out Dr. Bohart, the bee specialist needed assistance in transferring and relocating bee hives. I volunteered for two weekends and quit after getting stung several times.

ANIMAL HUSBANDRY AIDE

I heard about a weekend job assisting the Animal Husbandry department sampling cow abdomens treated with antibiotics to test their effectiveness. Their abdomens were surgically fitted with a screw cap lid. The lid was removed, samples taken with a small ladle and the lid screwed back on. One weekend of this testing was enough for me.

SORORITY HOUSE HASHING

A job to die for. Work included making the place settings, serving the meals and busing and washing the dishes. Besides getting free breakfasts and thirty dollars a week, the big bonus was meeting a lot of co-eds. The sorority tradition was to invite the hashers to their fall, winter and spring proms. While some of the inviters were not the most desirable dates – well you know – it was fun to attend the gatherings.

I hashed one year at the Sigma Kappa House and one year at the Chi Omega House next door. Two very memorable jobs.

USDA ANIMALS AFFECTING MAN AND ANIMALS

In the summer between my junior and senior years I worked for the government on two projects. The first project in Evanston, Wyoming was an anaplasmosis blood study involving a cattle disease. The source of the carrier was not known but suspected to be carried by either fleas, ticks or horseflies. My job was to harvest animals which carried these parasites, i.e., jack rabbits, ground squirrels and badgers. Once animals were harvested, they were placed in bags laced with chloroform to collect the parasites. The parasites were labeled and sent to the lab for analysis.

Collecting fly samples involved setting traps with an attractant. Traps were spread over a seven square mile area and samples collected once a week. Traps were checked on horseback. It took a good part of the day to collect, bag and label the samples which were also sent to a lab for analysis. I usually ended up with a sore ass after these horseback collections.

The second portion of this summer job involved testing chemicals as systematic mosquito repellents in mammals. Studies included collecting about 10,000 mosquitoes every two to three days. Collecting mosquitoes in flooded alfalfa was sometimes treacherous. The mosquitoes were so thick they produced a black cloud when disturbed. Usually, two or three net swipes were enough to collect adequate numbers for testing and getting out of Dodge as quickly as possible. Even though dosed with mosquito repellent, bites were common.

In the lab, mice were injected with a chemical, put in a small container with a screen on top and exposed to feeding mosquitoes. The end point consisted of examining blood-engorged mosquitoes. If engorged, the chemical was deemed an ineffective repellent candidate; chemicals from non-engorged mosquitoes were candidates for further testing.

SERENDIPITY

I omitted the circumstances that prevailed from meeting Patty. In the late fall of my second year at Berkeley, I had just failed my doctorate oral exam and was very depressed. To relieve my mental state, I opted to fly to Oil City and spend the holidays in an environment that would help me recover from my agony.

I said hell, I'll stop in Denver and drive to Colorado Springs to spend a couple days with Tom Robinson. He lived in an apartment complex as did his girlfriend. Turns out his girlfriend's roommate was Patty. It was love at first site. After a few days of partying, I flew to Oil City to spend a couple days with family. I only stayed three days and headed to Havana, Illinois where Patty was from.

After the first night of drinking, I ended up on the couch of my future in-laws. I awoke the next morning, and in sequence, saw two pairs of eyes staring at me (her two young nieces) followed by another set of two eyes belonging to her parents and followed by a third set of eyes belonging to her sister and brother-in-law. The adage you only get one chance to make a first impression didn't go well.

Thankfully, it's not the first impression that counts it's the last one that does. Luckily the last impression prevailed with my in-laws.

STUDENT LOANS

Touchy subject.

Perhaps you surmised that I was always broke – which I was. I never saved money and spent everything I earned just to survive. The reason I raise the issue of student loans is that the government is advocating partial or full forgiveness of student loans.

I don't agree with the proposal. I had three student loans in college. In order to finish my studies. I borrowed $200 from Utah State in my junior year to finish the school year. Had I not received this loan, I would have had to drop out of school and finish my degree at a later date.

The scholarship money I got in graduate school at Oregon State turned out to be inadequate to live on and support my lifestyle. I was forced to borrow $1,500 to complete my graduate work.

Likewise at Berkeley I borrowed $2,000 to finish my studies. All in all. I borrowed a total of $3,700. The value of my loans in the late fifties and sixties are equivalent to about $30K in today's dollars. All repayments started being due after finishing my studies. It took me 10 years to repay the loans. Believe me it was a struggle during that ten-year period.

I believe the government forgiveness loan payback program is unfair to students like me who paid off their loans and to those who did not go to college. Perhaps the students who borrowed money didn't believe they should pay it back. So, I'm not sympathetic with the notion that any portion of student loans should be forgiven.

Like Senator Kennedy from Louisiana said - if you borrowed the money, you pay it back.

COLLEGE STUDENT DRINKING

Again, I couldn't find a chronological sequence to include this topic so here it is.

While I did drink a lot on weekends in high school, I continued to do so in my college days.

A. Utah State

Utah has a notoriety for being a dry state – big joke. Utah Universities were also considered to be dry. My experiences state otherwise.

Basically, I only drank on weekends. Most of my frat brothers, especially, the older ones on the G.I. Bill, frequented the Cactus Club several nights a week. I didn't drink during the week mainly because I couldn't afford to.

My drinks of choice, besides beer, were Golden Spur and Thunderbird wines – mainly because they sold for one dollar a bottle. Talk about a cheap drunk. The wines were so vile to drink at normal temperatures. So, during the winter time, my roommate Lew Coons and I would bury the bottles in a mound of dirt and in a couple of hours until they were very cold and made drinking them somewhat tolerable.

In the spring quarter of my freshman year, I had a part-time job on Saturday doing cleaning university buildings. The work included cleaning rest rooms and polishing floors. Working hours were from 8-12 in the mornings. The job was fine – my head was not - especially after a night of drinking the cheap wines. Thank God the job only lasted three months.

B. Oregon State University

I was a graduate student and spent a lot of time in the lab doing research. However, I made some friends at the Sigma Nu Fraternity (of which I was a Member at Utah State) and occasionally drank with them. During my lab research, I befriended Jerry Blankenship (also a graduate student) – and we became roommates. Turns out he was a member of the Delta Upsilon fraternity. Through Jerry I met several DUs and spent much time with them.

One of the DUs, Tom Robinson, was a townie from Corvallis. Apparently, he was well known in local circles. I recall a party I was invited to early in my arrival to Corvallis. The party was moving along smoothly when suddenly a convertible GTO with four occupants pulled up outside and the girls yelled "Oh no its's the Robinsons" - Tom, brother Jay and two semi-social outcasts friends. The girls tried but were unable to lock the door - enter the Robinsons. Needless to say, the party quickly disbanded. I mention this episode because this was my first but not last encounter with Tom Robinson.

I eventually got to befriend Tom and did a lot of drinking and partying with him. After leaving Corvallis and heading for my graduate studies at Berkeley I thought I'd seen the last of Tom. Not so.

One day while at Berkeley I got a call from Tom. Turns out he got a lumber salesman job in San Jose, about 40 minutes from Berkeley. We routinely hooked up on the weekends and did some serious drinking and partying. Tom and I would meet on Friday evenings and part company on Sunday afternoon after a heavy nonstop weekend of drinking and partying. Thank God the weekend fun ended after a couple months with Tom getting a salesman job with Weyerhauser Lumber and moved to Denver. I definitely thought I saw the last of Tom. Not so.

DRUG DEALING

Again, I couldn't find an appropriate section to insert the following and I wanted to relay this occurrence to illustrate my stupidity. While graduate students at Oregon State, my second roommate Geoffrey Cheung and I had adjacent connected laboratories and both of us spent a lot of time in the lab doing research. As it turns out, we had access and authority to order chemicals for our research.

We shared the services of a lab assistant named Jim W. who was from Portland. Sort of an intelligent character but shady and hippy like. Somehow the subject of drugs, cocaine and their street value arose. Jim said he had contacts in Portland who could unload any cocaine he could get his hands on. Jeff and I thought we could make a few dollars if we could get our hands on cocaine. Problem we couldn't order cocaine since it was on the Federal Controlled Substance List and impossible for the layman to obtain the material from the manufacturer. However, the University was exempt from the Act and had the privileged of using cocaine for research purposes. While graduate students could order most research chemicals without a professor's signature, cocaine was not one of them.

We told Jim we might be able to order a pound. He said the street value for this amount was about $2,000. We agreed that if he peddled the drug our money share of the sale was one-half and he would get the other half. The money sounded good to us destitute graduate students. However, it was a very risky situation because if caught we would likely be expelled from graduate school. It was also likely the Feds might piggy back additional pain on us. Nonetheless Geoffrey ordered the drug forging our major professor's signature.

Talk about being apprehensive. The cocaine arrived as ordered. Jim said he would peddle the drug this coming weekend and see us on Monday with our share of the cash. Guess what – we never saw Jim again. All that risk for nothing.

UC BERKELEY GRADUATE SCHOOL

I was a PhD graduate student at U.C. Berkely under the direction of Dr. John Casida, a widely known scientist whose specialty was the metabolism and mode of action of agricultural chemicals as well as neurotoxic agents.

How my tenure at Berkeley came about was a kumbaya. While at Oregon State I became interested in the metabolism and mode of action of pesticides. Many of the top research papers on this subject were authored by Dr. Casida. I was having an issue at Oregon State in continuing my degree in Biochemistry.

So, on a whim I called Dr. Casida and told him of my interest in pesticides and said I would like to do graduate work under his direction. He asked me a few questions about my research background and said he would get back to me. Two days later he called and offered me a Fellowship. To say that I was elated was beyond words. To be able to attend one of the greatest universities in the country and work under one of the most recognized toxicologists in the country – if not in the world – made my day!

Looking back, it was interesting how Dr. Casida decided to offer me a Fellowship was initially somewhat of a mystery to me. I wasn't great academically but my research project at Oregon State was excellent. I later found out that one of the professors on my graduate committee, Dr. Newburgh, was a transfer professor from the University of Wisconsin – who served there on the faculty with Dr. Casida. To this day I believe the two collaborated and Dr. Newburgh provided a recommendation which resulted in the offer from Dr. Casida. Another kumbaya for me.

TOM ROBINSON – REMEMBER HIM?

During my second year of graduate school, I decided to go home to Oil City for Christmas. I said what the hell, I would stop and see Tom, who worked in Denver but lived in Colorado Springs. The girl he was dating was a school teacher who lived in the same apartment complex. Turns out she had a college roommate name Patty who was also a school teacher. I'll omit the details but I was introduced to Patty and it was love at first sight. Patty and I married one year later! Thank you, Tom. He was the best man at my wedding.

DR. CASIDA – A MENTOR

I was going to work hard to take advantage of my phenomenal opportunity at Berkeley. Unbeknownst to me, Dr. Casida had much to do with my success. He had an uncanny ability to subtly encourage me to work diligently and effectively in my research. But most of all he represented the father figure I never had. He had confidence in me and my work and I reciprocated and worked extra hard with my project. He provided the fatherly encouragement which was previously lacking in growing up. Our associations were not social in nature; the interactions were primarily research oriented. However, it was a win-win situation for both of us – I finally had a father figure who encouraged me and he got research publications from my work. I loved the man!

One memorable event while a graduate student at Berkeley had to do with my draft status. I had a 2S-student deferment from the draft which meant I was exempt from the draft as long as I was academically enrolled in college. The caveat was that I had to annually notify the Oil City Draft Board of my college enrollment status. It was in my second year of graduate work when I received a letter from Uncle Sam stating "Greetings we command you to report for the draft".

I was stunned as I had no desire to enlist in the service at this time and wished to finish my graduate research. Apparently, the reason for the letter was that I neglected to notify the Draft Board of my college status as required and they hunted me down in Berkeley. If drafted, I might not finish my goal for a PhD.

Thinking this was the end of my graduate studies, in panic, I rushed to Dr. Casida and showed him the letter. He said "let me have the letter and I'll see if there is anything I can do". Two weeks later, I received a letter from my Draft Board advising that my 2S-deferment was restored. Don't know how he did it but apparently the right strings were pulled. It was a case of who knows who.

Bit another bullet.

As an aside, after completing my graduate studies at 28 years of age my local Draft Board no longer recruited candidates at this age since there was an abundant pool of younger draft eligible males signed up with the Board.

HARVARD SCHOOL OF PUBLIC HEALTH

After receiving my PhD from Berkeley, I applied and received a Research Fellowship from Harvard. I was highly excited for the award. Metabolism and mode of action of drugs were the research studies – right up my level of expertise.

However, things were not as envisioned in my stint in Boston. Firstly, the teaching job my wife interviewed for didn't materialize. A week prior to arriving in Boston she was informed that the job was not available as promised. A professional setback for me revolved around the instrumentation I was promised but because of funding did not arrive. I still was able to conduct interesting research without the analytical instruments but not in depth as I hoped. After 18 months of Boston, I was glad to leave Harvard.

PROFESSIONAL EXPERIENCE

Hard to believe but even with the most coveted academic training and credentials, I was unable to find a position after Harvard because of the tight job market. At that time, I was probably one of only ten toxicologists in the country - in high demand or so I thought. I was initially interviewed and offered a position teaching chemistry at the University of Alaska. I was salivating at the potential of the outdoor hunting and fishing opportunities. However, after deliberations with my wife, and weighing the pros and cons of the daylight pattern, I declined the offer.

I then was offered a position with the Department of Agriculture Chemistry Pesticide Metabolism Unit in Fargo, North Dakota. The hang up here was government policies: they had the job opening but didn't have the money to fill the position. They promised they would deliver a contract but it didn't happen.

I subsequently applied for a position with the U.S. Fish and Wildlife Research Institute in Denver – a prize if there ever was one. Again, government politics prevented them from making a job offer. They had the money but no official position. Our government in action.

Quite frustrated at the time and running low on funds, I told Patty I would accept the first offer I receive. Out of the blue, I received a call from a head hunter in San Francisco who said he had an opening for a toxicologist with a chemical company in Richmond,

California. Needless to say, I jumped at the opportunity and took the job. How they found me was an enigma. Found out later Dr. Casida recommended me for the position.

For the next 27 years I was titled as a Senior Research Toxicologist. Worked three years for Stauffer Chemical, 24 years for Chevron Chemical Company, both for the Agricultural Chemical and the ORTHO Garden and Home Pesticide Divisions and two years for Monsanto Chemicals. I was responsible for regulatory human toxicology and fish and wild safety field studies. I did a lot of traveling during my job and met many wonderful people. During my employment I visited all states in the lower 48 except for West Virginia; I was as close as 30 miles from their border. I also got approximately 40 airline travel award tickets from my travels. Our family used the awards and did a lot of traveling to DC (3 times), Disney World, Texas and several family reunions.

While I had no plan to retire at age 59 our Chevron business was sold to an Ohio firm. I had an option to relocate or retire. I chose the latter. I had no desire to go back East. I retired April 1, 1999. Happy April Fool's Day!

TROPHY BUSINESS

Again, I couldn't find a convenient chronological mention of the business I started up while employed full time by Chevron Chemical. I insert it here to give you a flavor of the rat race I was involved in for a period of time. So here it is.

Money was always short while raising a family of three boys in California – and still paying off my student loans. Patty didn't teach while our boys were growing up so we had to live on my salary – which never seemed adequate. I tried several side jobs on weekends when the boys were young. I soon gave up side job hunting in frustration.

Eventually I got hooked on youth baseball not because I wanted to but because I had to. The league was short of coaches. The choice was either I manage a team or my son doesn't play. I chose the latter. Ended up coaching youth baseball for 15 years with each of my three sons.

Getting back to finances. Having trouble meeting family expenses, I still needed an additional source of income in addition to my regular job. Here comes baseball again. Our baseball league needed Board Members; I was coerced into serving. The league awarded numerous first place and participation trophies. After looking into money our league paid for trophies, I started up a garage trophy business. I was able to sway our Board in purchasing trophies and awards from me. I also hustled business from other leagues we interacted with. In no time I had a booming business.

Now I was super busy with my full-time job, coaching baseball and doing trophies. I did trophies from 4 AM until 7 AM, went to work from 8 AM–4:30 PM, did baseball from 5-8 PM, followed by evening trophy assembly from 8 PM until midnight. My tongue was hanging out but I persevered.

However, I had plenty of local labor; Patty did much of the engraving and my boys as well as a few neighbor kids assembled trophies. I did trophies for 8 years. One of the happiest days of my life besides meeting Patty, getting married and having kids was selling the business! Forgot to mention other super happy days occurred each time I sold one of the ten boats I owned.

UNIVERSITY OF CALIFORNIA
MEDICAL SCHOOL

Ten years after retirement, I still had the itch to do laboratory research. I applied for and got hired by the University of California Medical Center in Sacramento to do neurological research with extremely toxic drugs. The mode of action of these drugs were not clear but it was known they did affect the brain. In order to elucidate the metabolism and mode of action in mammas radiolabeled drugs were used in animal research.

The research was very challenging. It was exactly the type of research for which I was trained. We did make several key observations from my research. However, just when the research was promising and we were making breakthroughs, my tenure was terminated after four years when our Research Grant was not renewed. I haven't done any laboratory research work since then. What a bummer.

MEETING U.S. PRESIDENTS

RONALD REAGAN

ACTOR RONALD RERAGAN ARRIVES AT THE FIELDHOUSE CEREMONIES

During college I had the opportunity to be photographed with then president Ronald Reagan in my senior year of college. See picture above. Our Fraternity, the Sigma Nu, presented and directed under the auspices of Utah State University, our annual "Oscar Awards". Participation in the plays was mandatory for all frat members who in one way or another were participated in the event. The Oscar program emulated Hollywood and included presentation awards to Professor of the Year, Student of the Year, Athlete of the Year, etc. Dignitaries were invited to briefly address the audience. The awards were preceded by a short play presented by our fraternity members and a few sorority females. The first year the presentation was "West Side Story" followed by the second year of "South Pacific". In my sophomore year I had a bit part as a gang member pleading with Officer Krumski. In my junior year I was a singing sailor in South Pacific. Needless to say, participation in the event was a lot of work and cut into one's social life; it was especially a monumental endeavor when participation was required without exception.

In my senior year I was a serious student and refused to participate in any Oscar events because of my studies. Finally, I caved and was delegated to opening the doors of limos for the celebrities who included Ronald Reagan then Governor of California, and Chill Willis. Enclosed is a photograph of me with Ronald Reagan while opening the door of his limo as he arrived in a limo for the Oscars. Can't remember who gave me the photo but it was something I cherish to this day.

GEORGE H. WALKER BUSH, THE ELDER

While I did not get photographed with President George W. Bush, I did have an opportunity to shake his hand. This occurred in an upscale D.C. Italian restaurant. I was seated with six other Chevron managers who had attended a high value meeting with the EPA to discuss issues with a pesticide. It was weird – when we entered the restaurant, the owner appeared extremely nervous and was pacing around constantly looking out the front door. Shortly after we were seated and unbeknown to us, a contingency of Secret

Service men covering the President entered the restaurant and were heading into a room in the rear reserved for the President and his party. As it turns out, I was close to the aisle where he would pass by and as he did pass by, I excitedly jumped up, reached out my hand and shook his. I think the President was shocked as I was. Immediately, the Secret Service surrounded the President – and me! Momentarily I thought the Service was going to take me down – but didn't. President Bush shook my hand, said "hello how are you" and proceeded to the back room.

POLISH COOKING - AFTER THOUGHTS

My mom from Pennsylvania would visit us in California once a year. When she visited, I would literally chain her to the kitchen and demand she cook us Polish foods. Truth is she always enjoyed cooking for Naniu, my Polish nickname. We all relished the food she cooked, even my picky eater son Greg. As time went on, I asked her to copy recipes for me which to this date I retained.

From following her recipes, I honed my Polish culinary skills. On occasions I cook many of these ethnic dishes. In fact, I annually hosted a Polish dinner for friends where I now live. It's of interest that none of these folks have tasted Polish food except for kielbasa (Polish sausage) purchased from local grocery stores. To maintain authenticity in my dinners, I ordered Polish foods, that I couldn't prepare myself, from either Chicago or Philadelphia. My Polish dinners were fully enjoyed by my guests. The prepared dishes were abundant and guests always request several dishes to take home.

My signature prepared Polish foods are pierogi, similar to Chinese pot stickers. They are fried to a golden brown in butter rather than steamed or fried in oil. The pierogi are filled with either a potato/cheese mix or sauerkraut thoroughly rinsed and fried in butter. They're a lot of work to prepare but well worth the effort – they are to die for!

Sad to say there are no Polish Restaurants in the Northern California. The only Polish restaurant, The Warsawa, was in Berkeley. However, it closed about 30 years ago probably due to the lack of demand. There are, however, several Polish delis in the Area but it's not the same experience as a full sit-down restaurant. Besides they don't offer many ethnic items I prepare.

REGRESSING AND REMINISCING

To this day I wonder what twists and turns would have changed if I was raised with a father. I now reflect on my grandsons and their situations with tears in my eye – tears of happiness - since all seven of my grandkids have been and are being properly mentored by their parents. I made it a point to spend time with my three sons; I wanted to be sure they had support and guidance which I didn't have. I spent 15 years as their coach in youth baseball. I wouldn't trade the experience for anything in the world. I took them tent camping fishing and even started them in hunting ducks, deer and turkeys.

My eldest son lives in San Mateo, California and his two boys are doing great. Matthew, the oldest, went to a highly rated private high school, graduated with a 4.0+ grade point. In his junior and senior years, he tutored students for a fee and has worked part-time as a waiter and maître de in an upscale pricey restaurant. He's was very happy with the generous tips he received from his patrons. He's now enrolled as a freshman at Loyola Marymount University in Los Angeles as a business major.

His younger brother Dominic, who likewise has excellent grades, enrolled as a freshman in Serra High School. Dominic plays youth soccer and basketball and does quite well. He recently was invited to a goalie competition in Florida. He didn't take first but his skills were very evident.

My middle son Greg who lives in Woodland, California, has a daughter named Kayleigh currently enrolled as a junior in Clemson, doing very well academically. She's a videographer for the Varsity Football Program at the University.

His son Waylon, and daughter Natalie, ages seven and six, respectively, are doing very well academically in Woodland Christian. Their parents spend an inordinate amount of time with them. Wayland plays basketball, is in his second year of baseball and has started soccer this fall.

My youngest son Chris. Lives in Washington, Illinois His daughter Sophie, who is a senior year in high school, played youth basketball, is a varsity cheer leader, ran track and excels academically. She hopes to attend the University of Illinois as did her parents.

Her brother Luke started high school this year. Parochial school grades were great. He loves sports. Luke played youth hockey, baseball and his favorite sport basketball. He's trying out for the freshman basketball team.

My sons spend a lot of time with their children. Bottom line: if parents spend time with their sons and daughters, keep them busy with academics, sports, etc. they likely will turn out to be outstanding kids – as seems to be the case with my grandkids.

Again, I wonder how or what my life what would have been if I had a dad.

As an aside, I instilled into my sons the benefits and rewards of hard work. Each of my sons played high school sports; i.e., baseball, basketball and football. Each of them also worked part-time for Longs Drugs during their entire high school days. Longs was very accommodating with flexible schedules for their athletic activities. With the trophy money and their drug store savings, they all saved enough money to buy their own first cars.

REFLECTIONS

And there it is folks. Even with a few bumps in the road, life was good because of my determination and work ethic. In retrospect, I truly have no regrets of any decisions made in my lifetime (maybe a couple) or the pathways they led me to. Many men on their death beds say they wished they would have spent more time with their family. In my case, it's the opposite - I wished I would have spent more time dedicated to my career!

Bottom line – no life regrets.

CPSIA information can be obtained
at www.ICGtesting.com
Printed in the USA
BVHW081218301222
655311BV00007B/479